BIBLE CRAFTS
FOR HOLIDAYS

By
Susan J. Stegenga

Illustrated by Darcy Tom

Cover by Darcy Tom

Copyright © 1994

Shining Star Publications

ISBN No. 0-86653-770-8

Standardized Subject Code TA ac

Printing No. 98765432

Shining Star Publications
1204 Buchanan St., Box 299
Carthage, IL 62321-0299

The purchase of this book entitles the buyer to reproduce student activity pages for classroom use only. Any other use requires written permission from Shining Star Publications.

All rights reserved. Printed in the United States of America.

Unless otherwise indicated, the New International Version of the Bible was used in preparing the activities in this book.

DEDICATION

This book is dedicated to some special little people: Audrey, Sarah, Gary, Ryan, Heidi, Christopher, Mikela, Gavin, Levi, Caleb, John Charles (Juan Carlos), and their parents.

It's exciting watching all of you grow up as the next generation. May God bless you with friends as wonderful as your parents have been to me over the years.

Also, thanks again to my parents and editor Becky Daniel for your ongoing support and encouragement.

TABLE OF CONTENTS

To the Teacher/Parent 4

NEW YEAR'S DAY
Painted Glass Plaque 5
Balloon Pop-Up Card 6
Prayer Calendar 9
Family Resolutions–Balloon Magnets 10
Prayer Journal 11

VALENTINE'S DAY
Jewelry Treasure Box 12
Heart "Sun Catcher" 13
Victorian Lace Doily–Hanging Valentine...14
Victorian-Style Collage Pin
   and Greeting Card 15
Love Bookmark......................................16
Heart Wall Hanging 17
Heart Key Holder 18
Heart Picture Frame 19
Country-Style Heart Wreath 20
Calico Quilt Heart–Notepad Holder 21
Teddy Bear Card 22
Valentine Puzzle Card 25

PALM SUNDAY
Palm Sunday Puppet–Shoe Box Stage 26

EASTER
Cross Silhouette Painting 28
"Stained Glass Window"
   and Cross Magnet 29
Pressed Flowers–Easter Bookmark 30
"Stained Glass Window" Cookies............31
Easter Plant-Pick Decoration 32
Easter "Son"rise Flowerpot....................33
Easter "Son"rise Mobile 34
Crayon Batik Easter Wind Sock 37
Easter Butterfly Mobile or Card 38

MOTHER'S DAY
Mother's Bulletin Board 40
Pencil or Kitchen Utensil Holder 41
"Fruits of the Spirit"
   Recipe Box and Cards 42
"Country Charm" Mobile 43
Mom's "Treat" Jar 46
Potpourri Sachet 47
Lace Doily Basket..................................48
A Special Mom's T-shirt 49
Mom's Framed Mirror 50
Mom's Tote Bag 52
Flower Pop-Up Card 54

FATHER'S DAY
Crayon Batik Handkerchief.....................56
Computer Floppy Disk File 57
Dad's TV Remote Control Holder 58
Dad's Note Clips/Bookmarks 60
Dad's Sweatshirt and Cap 61
Sports Water Bottle...............................62
Dad's Chef or Carpentry Apron 63
Hand-Painted "Power" Necktie 64
Dad's Tie Rack 65
Dad's Decorated Coat Hanger.................66
Father's Day Award Certificate 67

THANKSGIVING
Class Thanksgiving Mural 69
Autumn Leaves Wall Hanging 70
Thanksgiving Praise Tree 71
Thanksgiving Magnets...........................72
Thanksgiving Felt Banner 73
Miniature Harvest Wreath 74
Thanksgiving Food Sculptures 75
Thanksgiving Miniature Centerpiece 76
Thanksgiving Napkin Holders 77
Turkey Nut Cups 78
Thanksgiving Place Cards 79
Thanksgiving Place Mats.......................80

CHRISTMAS
Advent Calendar 81
Advent Wreath 84
Manger Scene Mailbox 86
Christmas Guests Hand Towel 87
Paper Plate Mobile 88
Nativity Scene Figures..........................90
Styrofoam™ Cup Nativity Animals 91
Christmas Lamb Card............................92
Stiffened Fabric Ornaments and Gifts 95

CREATIVITY AWARD CERTIFICATE.........96

TO THE TEACHER/PARENT

The holiday projects suggested in this book are intended to be made and used in Christian education settings, such as Sunday school, children's church, youth club, Christian day school, and the home. Permission is given to reproduce patterns for use in these settings. Reproduce patterns by using copy machines, carbon paper, or basic tracing methods.

The project ideas are intended to be general guidelines and springboards for creativity. Be flexible in planning and using the projects according to your situation. The projects can easily be interchanged for different holidays; for example, you might plan to use a Valentine's Day gift idea for Mother's Day or vice versa.

Be sensitive to the home situation of each child. For example, if a child is being raised by grandparents, encourage that child to make gifts for grandparents on Mother's and Father's Days (or celebrate Grandparents' Day). Also, remember that many children live in single-parent homes and may have very little or no contact with the other parent. If that is the case, encourage the child to make a gift for another male or female friend or relative for Mother's or Father's Day if that particular parent is absent from the child's life.

Try not to stereotype when using the projects, although certain projects have been listed in categories. If Dad is the cook in the family, a child may make a recipe box for him. If Mom is the athlete, the child may make the "sports pattern" projects for her.

Instructions are written to help each child complete the project successfully. Keep this in mind if you work with a group. Plan according to the needs of the individual children with whom you work. Some projects are easier and require less time and fewer materials than others. Choose projects which are appropriate for each child's skill level and attention span.

Before beginning each project, read through the directions carefully, and discuss the illustrations to make sure each child understands. Encourage the child to choose what colors of materials to use. Gather other supplies and organize an appropriate work area. If using materials that might spill such as paint, protect the work area with newspapers and cover each child's clothing with an apron or a large, old shirt.

Except when safety is a factor and an adult's supervision or assistance is recommended, encourage each child to do as much of the work as possible without your intervention. Have fun!

PAINTED GLASS PLAQUE

"Therefore, if anyone is in Christ, he is a new creation; the old has gone, the new has come!"
2 Corinthians 5:17

MATERIALS:
Precut, beveled edge glass (approximately 7" x 7")
Craft or glass paint in bright or shiny metallic colors and black (in squeeze bottles)
Colorful sequins or metallic confetti
Craft glue
$1\frac{1}{2}$" x $3\frac{1}{2}$" piece of wood (approximately 7" long with a $\frac{1}{4}$" wide and $\frac{1}{2}$" deep groove)
Black or brown liquid shoe polish
Clear spray varnish
Newspapers

INSTRUCTIONS:
1. Paint three brightly colored balloon shapes on the glass.
2. Let the balloons dry; then outline them with black paint. Paint "God bless you!" on the balloons, one word on each.
3. Paint your name and the new year's date near the bottom corner of the glass.
4. Glue sequins or metallic confetti around the balloons.
5. Stain the wood with shoe polish. Let it dry.
6. Place the wood on newspapers. Ask an adult to help you spray it with clear varnish in a well-ventilated area.
7. After the plaque and wood are both dry, place the plaque in the groove in the wood to display.
8. Give the plaque to someone to wish him or her God's blessings in the new year.

HELPFUL HINTS AND OTHER IDEAS:
- You can purchase beveled glass pieces at a stained glass supply store. If you have a large class, you may be able to purchase beveled glass in bulk packages of approximately thirty pieces.
- An adult will need to grind all unbeveled edges to make sure there are no sharp edges. People who work in glass shops are often glad to do this, if they know it's for a class project.
- An adult will need to cut a $\frac{1}{4}$" wide groove approximately $\frac{1}{2}$" deep on the block of wood. People who work at lumberyards may be willing to help with this procedure.
- Use a mirror tile instead of glass for a reflective background.

BALLOON POP-UP CARD

Start the new year by wishing a friend or relative God's special blessings!

MATERIALS:
Balloon card patterns, pages 7-8
Glue stick
Crayons, markers, or colored pencils
Craft glue
Scissors
Decorative trims (glitter glue, metallic or paper confetti, sequins, colorful stickers, foil stars, yarn, etc.)

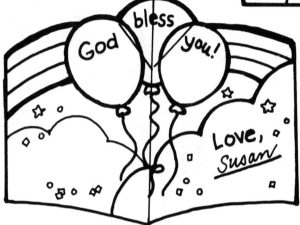

INSTRUCTIONS:
1. Copy the patterns on pages 7-8. If possible, use a two-sided copy machine so the patterns can be copied on the front and back of a single sheet of paper. Or reproduce the patterns on separate sheets of paper, and cut them out. Then use a glue stick to glue the sheets together back-to-back.
2. Trim the edges, and throw away the excess.
3. Fold along the broken line in the middle.
4. Fold down on the V-shape; then open the card.
5. Reverse the direction of the vertical fold in the top V-section by pushing it to the inside.
6. Holding the folded side of the card with one hand, pinch the pop-up portion on the inside and pull down. As you pull down and press, the card will fold properly.
7. Color the inside and outside of the card.
8. Glue yarn on the balloon strings and other trims such as confetti or sequins on the card.
9. You may want to use glitter glue to write the year on the balloons.
10. After the card dries, sign your name on the blank line on the inside. Send or give the card to wish someone a happy new year!

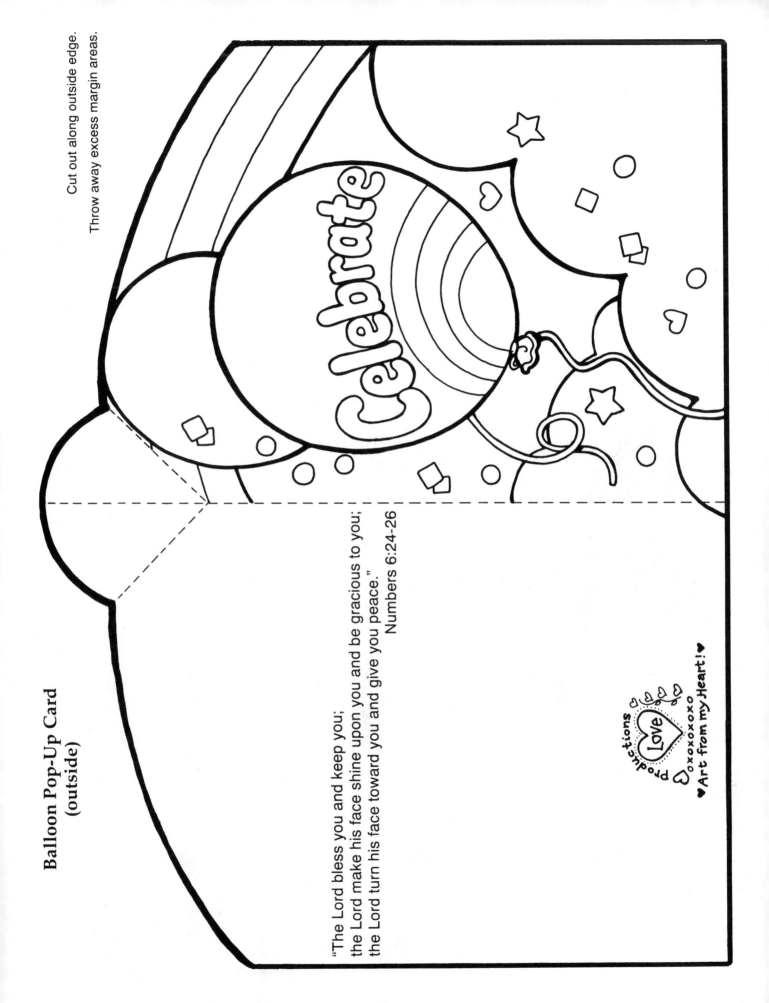

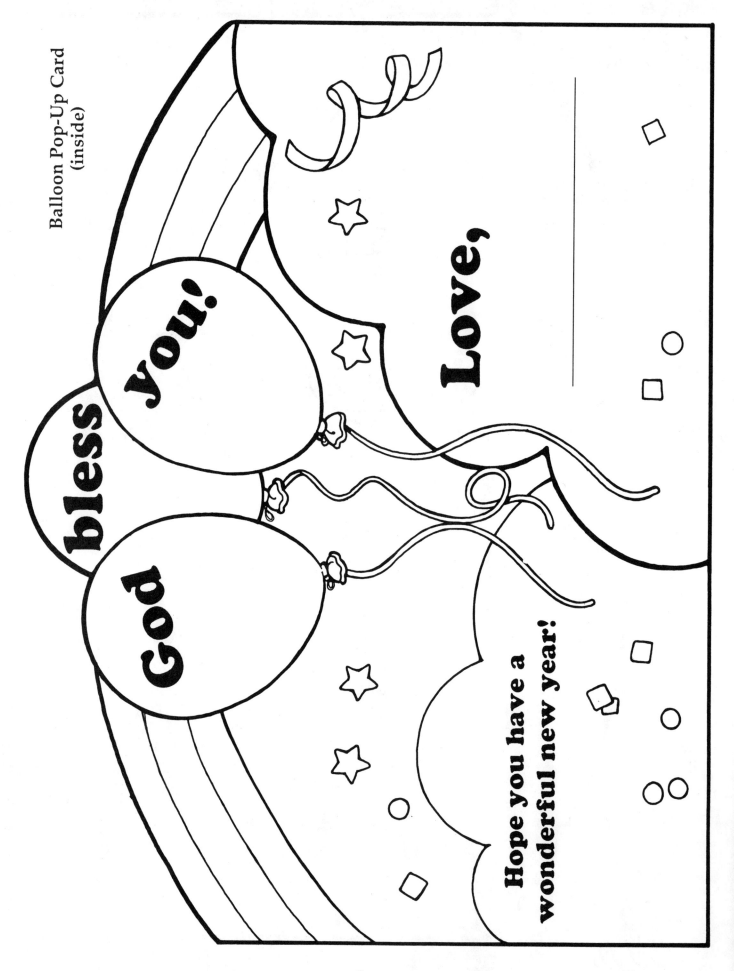

PRAYER CALENDAR

"Pray continually." 1 Thessalonians 5:17

MATERIALS:
Large calendar
Magazine pictures
Scissors
Glue
Construction paper
Markers or crayons
Yarn
Tape

INSTRUCTIONS:
1. Begin with a large calendar (these can be purchased inexpensively or are given away at local businesses).
2. Decide on a prayer topic for each month, such as missionaries, church programs, family needs, or friends.
3. Cover the calendar pictures with construction paper.
4. Illustrate the monthly topics by cutting out magazine pictures or cutting designs from construction paper. Add details with markers or crayons. Glue the pictures on the construction paper.
5. Label the pictures with prayer topics. You also may want to choose weekly subtopics—missionary safety, missionary health, or spreading the Gospel.
6. Draw a small box on each day to check as you and your family pray for the topics (make notes of answered prayers).
7. Tape yarn to the calendar to hang it up.

OTHER IDEA:
- Make a calendar rather than using a premade one. Look at a premade calendar to copy the proper dates under the days of the week.

FAMILY RESOLUTIONS BALLOON MAGNETS

"The mind controlled by the Spirit is life and peace." Romans 8:6b
"Therefore be clear minded and self-controlled so that you can pray." 1Peter 4:7b

MATERIALS:
Lightweight craft foam rubber (in different colors)
Scissors
Fine-line black marker
Yarn or string
Craft glue
Magnets or magnetic tape
Typing paper

INSTRUCTIONS:
1. Cut from craft foam a different colored balloon shape for each member of your family.
2. Write the name of a family member on each balloon.
3. Glue yarn or string to the back of each balloon as shown in the illustration. Let glue dry thoroughly.
4. Attach a magnet or piece of magnetic tape to the back of each balloon.
5. Cut small strips of typing paper and give one to each family member.
6. Ask each person to write down a resolution of something he or she will try to do better this year, with God's help. Examples of resolutions include praying each night, reading the Bible daily, etc. Or family members can choose and write down Bible verses to memorize.
7. Post resolutions or memory verses on the refrigerator using the balloon magnets. Pray together and help each other keep these resolutions or memorize the verses. Change the slips of paper on a regular basis, such as weekly.

HELPFUL HINTS AND OTHER IDEAS:
- You can buy small bags containing scraps of different colored craft foam at many hobby and craft stores.
- Rather than using foam rubber, make balloons from construction paper and cover them with clear adhesive plastic.

PRAYER JOURNAL

"We constantly pray for you." 2 Thessalonians 1:11a

MATERIALS:
Notebook with lined paper (pocket size or notebook size)
Small pen or sharpened pencil
Fabric
Scissors
Ribbon
Craft glue
Construction paper
Clear adhesive plastic
Decorative trims (lace, sequins, etc.)

INSTRUCTIONS:
1. Cut fabric or construction paper, and glue it on the outside of the notebook to cover it. If you're using fabric, overlap the edges of the material and glue them on the inside of the notebook cover, leaving enough slack so the notebook opens and closes easily. Let it dry.
2. Decorate the cover with scraps of paper, fabric, lace, sequins, etc.
3. On the front cover, write "Prayer Journal" (or "Diary") and the name of the person who will use it. If you're using construction paper, cover it with clear adhesive plastic to protect it.
4. Glue some ribbon on the sides, as shown, to tie the book shut. Tie a pen or pencil to the ribbon. Make sure the ribbon is long enough so the pen or pencil can be used to write in the journal.
5. Label the pages with months and dates.
6. Use this journal yourself, or give it to someone as a gift for the new year to write down daily prayer requests and record answers to prayer.

JEWELRY TREASURE BOX

"But store up for yourselves treasures in heaven . . . For where your treasure is, there your heart will be also."

Matthew 6:20a, 21

MATERIALS:
Round or cube-shaped box or metal (tin) container with lid
Fabric, wallpaper, or adhesive plastic with designs
Felt
Scissors
Construction paper
Decorative trims (beads, heart-shaped buttons, sequins, ribbons, artificial flowers, etc.)
Paint pens
Craft glue
Fine-line marker

INSTRUCTIONS:
1. Cover the container or box with fabric, wallpaper, or adhesive plastic.
2. Cut and glue felt to line the inside. Let it dry.
3. Cut a small heart from construction paper. Write the words "Love one another!" on it. Glue the heart to the outside of the treasure box.
4. Decorate the outside by using paint pens and trims.
5. On a slip of paper, write the words of Matthew 6:20a, 21. Put the slip of paper inside the treasure box.
6. Give this valentine gift to someone as a reminder of your love and of God's love, our greatest treasure. (Tell the person it's all right to store a few "earthly treasures" such as jewelry in this particular box.)

HEART "SUN CATCHER"

"For God, who said, 'Let light shine out of darkness,' made his light shine in our hearts."

2 Corinthians 4:6a

MATERIALS:
Low-temperature glue gun and glue sticks
Aluminum foil
Craft glue (precolored or tinted with food coloring or poster paint)
Glitter or glitter glue
String or transparent nylon fishline
Construction paper
Markers
Pencil
Scissors

INSTRUCTIONS:
1. With an adult's help, use a glue gun to make several lacy, "squiggly" designs on a large sheet of aluminum foil to look like round doilies or snowflakes.
2. After they dry, decorate the lacy designs to make heart shapes with colored craft glue and glitter. Write "Love" on one of the hearts.
3. After they dry, remove the glue designs from the foil.
4. Tie the designs together with string or fishline. Then tie string or fishline on the top piece to hang it up.
5. If you plan to give this sun catcher to someone, make a card from construction paper to go with it, and write the words "God's love shines down on us!" Explain to the person you give it to that this is a sun catcher, and if it is hung in a window, rays of sunlight will shine through it and brighten the area around it. Similarly, God sent Jesus to earth so His love could shine through us to everyone around us!

VICTORIAN LACE DOILY HANGING VALENTINE

"Love one another deeply, from the heart." 1 Peter 1:22b

MATERIALS:
Lace doilies (two or more)
Scissors
Glue
Red and pink construction paper scraps
Ribbon
Decorative trims (Victorian-style stickers or gift wrap decorated with angels or flowers, beads, heart stickers, tiny flowers made from ribbon, lace, shiny buttons, tiny pearls, glitter, etc.)
Fine-line markers
Hole punch
Paper

INSTRUCTIONS:
1. Glue two doilies together.
2. Cut a heart shape from construction paper or from another lace doily. Glue it on the other doilies, leaving the top open to form a small pocket.
3. Decorate the heart with trims. Cut little angels from gift wrap or add Victorian-style stickers to create an old-fashioned appearance.
4. Cut ribbon and prestrung pearls and glue them to the bottom of the project so they hang down as streamers.
5. Punch a hole at the top and tie a piece of ribbon through it so the heart can be hung up.
6. Write a love note on a slip of paper and tuck it into the heart pocket.
7. Give this valentine to someone you love.

OTHER IDEAS:
- Make extra pockets by gluing several layers of extra doilies of different sizes to the project.
- Dab a tiny bit of cologne on a small cotton ball. Tuck this into one of the pockets to make the valentine smell nice.

VICTORIAN-STYLE COLLAGE PIN AND GREETING CARD

"I have you in my heart."   Philippians 1:7a

(The Victorian period was during the 19th century when Queen Victoria reigned in England. People during that time exchanged beautiful cards to show their love. You, too, can make a pretty card and pin for someone special.)

MATERIALS:
Precut wooden or sturdy cardboard heart
Scissors
Acrylic paint (pink, red, or lavender)
Paintbrush
Large pin back or safety pin
Craft glue
Decorative trims (lace, ribbons, tiny ribbon roses, buttons, beads, strings of imitation pearls, little Victorian angel stickers or pictures cut from gift wrap, heart stickers, glitter, etc.)
Construction paper (pink, red, or lavender)
Lace doilies
Fine-line markers

INSTRUCTIONS:
1. Paint the wooden heart, or ask an adult to help you cut a heart shape out of cardboard to paint. Let the paint dry thoroughly.
2. Glue the pin to the back. Let it dry.
3. Decorate the heart with trims. Let the pin dry overnight.
4. Make a card by folding construction paper in half. Decorate by gluing on doilies. Write a greeting, such as "P.S. God loves you, and so do I!" or a Bible verse, such as Philippians 1:7a, inside the card.
5. Sign your name inside the card.
6. After the card dries, ask an adult to help you pin the decorated heart to the front.
7. Give the card to someone. Explain that the heart pin can be removed from the card and worn as a reminder of God's love and yours.

LOVE BOOKMARK

"God has poured out his love into our hearts . . . ."   Romans 5:5b

MATERIALS:
Wooden or sturdy cardboard heart
Scissors
Acrylic paints
Small paintbrush
Wide ribbon (approximately 1" wide and 9" long)
Fabric paint
Craft glue

INSTRUCTIONS:
1. Use a wooden heart, or ask an adult to help you cut a heart shape from cardboard.
2. Paint the heart, and let it dry.
3. Using a darker color, paint "God loves you!" on the heart.
4. Cut a piece of ribbon, and glue it to the back of the heart. Let it dry.
5. Paint small hearts on the ribbon, and let them dry.
6. Give the bookmark to someone as a gift, or use it as a Bible bookmark.

OTHER IDEA:
- Make the heart out of other materials, such as self-hardening clay or shrink art plastic that you bake in the oven with adult supervision. Follow the directions included with these products. You may purchase them at a craft or hobby store.

HEART WALL HANGING

"God is love."

1 John 4:16b

MATERIALS:
Three wooden or sturdy cardboard hearts
Acrylic paints
Paintbrush
Brass curtain ring
Scissors
Wide ribbon
Fabric paint (optional)
Craft glue

INSTRUCTIONS:
1. Cut a piece of ribbon about 15" long.
2. Thread one end of the ribbon through the brass ring, and glue. Let it dry.
3. Paint the wooden hearts and let them dry, or ask an adult to help you cut three heart shapes from cardboard and paint them.
4. After the first coat of paint is dry, use a darker color to paint "God is love!" or "Bless this home!" on the hearts, one word on each heart.
5. After the hearts have dried, glue them on the ribbon to make a wall hanging as shown.
6. Paint tiny hearts on the ribbon, if desired.
7. Hang this project in your home, or give it to someone as a gift.

HEART KEY HOLDER

"[Nothing] . . . will be able to separate us from the love of God that is in Christ Jesus our Lord."
Romans 8:39b

MATERIALS:
Flat 1/2" thick, 4" x 12" piece of plywood
Sandpaper
Acrylic paints
Paintbrushes or sponge brushes
Three small screw-on brass hooks
Two brass curtain rings
Low-temperature glue gun and glue sticks
Narrow ribbon

INSTRUCTIONS:
1. Ask an adult to cut a piece of plywood 4" x 12".
2. Sand the edges until they are smooth. (Be careful not to get splinters!)
3. Decide whether you want to make a horizontal or vertical plaque. If you make a vertical one, you will probably only need one large brass ring to hang it up.
4. Paint the board and let it dry.
5. Paint three or more large hearts on the board, and let them dry. For younger children refer to "other ideas."
6. Paint on the hearts, "Jesus holds the keys to my heart!" Let dry.
7. Paint tiny decorative hearts or another design for a border. Let dry.
8. Use a glue gun (or other strong glue) to attach the ring(s) to the back of the wood. (Adult help is recommended.) Let the glue dry thoroughly.
9. Tie decorative ribbons on the ring(s).
10. Ask an adult to help you screw three brass hooks on the hearts below the words.
11. Hang the key holder on the wall so that your family can hang their keys on it.

OTHER IDEAS:
- Rather than using paintbrushes, you may wish to use sponges cut into heart shapes to paint the design on the key holder, or paint over heart-shaped stencils made from cardboard or purchased at a craft store.
- Create an interesting effect by overlapping the hearts.

HEART PICTURE FRAME

"Dear friends, let us love one another, for love comes from God."   1 John 4:7a

MATERIALS:
Precut heart-shaped frame such as a mat board or sturdy cardboard
Scissors or hobby knife
Cotton print fabric and cotton batting (or patterned wallpaper, wrapping paper, colored adhesive plastic, or construction paper)
Craft glue
Decorative trims (ribbon, beads, lace, etc.)
Fabric paint
Photograph (friends, family members, etc.)
Transparent tape
Fine-line markers

INSTRUCTIONS:
1. Begin with a precut frame, or ask an adult to help you cut one.
2. If you're using a precut frame, cover it with lightweight batting (stuffing) and fabric to make a soft padded frame. Precut frames in fabric shops usually contain detailed instructions regarding how to do this. If you make your own frame, cut batting the size of the frame, remembering to cut an opening in front. Glue the batting on the cardboard. Cut the fabric slightly larger than the frame, and glue to the front. Notch the curved edges before folding and gluing the edges to the back side of the frame.
3. You may prefer to make an unpadded, flat frame by gluing fabric or paper directly to the frame. Trim the edges carefully.
4. Decorate the frame with trims.
5. Using fabric paint or markers, write a message such as "Love one another" on the frame.
6. Insert a favorite photo behind the frame, and tape it or glue it down.
7. Give the frame to someone as a valentine gift.

OTHER IDEAS:
- Add a triangular flap that folds back to the frame to make it stand up on a desk or shelf.
- Glue a magnetic strip behind a tiny frame so it can be displayed on a metal file cabinet or a refrigerator.
- Hang a tiny frame from a ribbon so the frame can dangle from the ceiling or be hung on the wall.
- Glue a small framed photo to a paper doily; then glue the doily on a valentine made from folded construction paper.

COUNTRY-STYLE HEART WREATH

"Love never fails." 1 Corinthians 13:8a

"His [the Lord's] love endures forever." Psalm 136:1b

MATERIALS:
Wooden craft hoop or a ring precut from sturdy cardboard or a plastic lid
Scissors
Lightweight cardboard or poster board
Low-temperature glue gun and glue sticks
Lightweight cotton fabric (coordinating prints in red or pink and white color schemes)
Decorative trims (coordinating colored ribbons, laces, heart-shaped buttons, etc.)
Craft glue
Black marker or fabric paint in squeeze bottle

INSTRUCTIONS:
1. Cut heart shapes in a variety of sizes from lightweight cardboard or poster board to fit on the ring.
2. Cover each heart with fabric, and glue in place. Trim edges of the fabric to fit the heart shapes.
3. Use a glue gun to glue the hearts on the ring to make a wreath. (Adult help is recommended.)
4. Use craft glue to add trims to the wreath.
5. Use a marker or fabric paint to write "God loves you!" on the wreath, putting each word on a different heart.
6. When the wreath has dried, attach a ribbon to hang it up.
7. Give the wreath to someone as a reminder that God's love never ends–it lasts forever!

CALICO QUILT HEART NOTEPAD HOLDER

"A new command I give you: Love one another. As I have loved you, so you must love one another."

John 13:34

MATERIALS:
Sturdy cardboard
Scissors
Pinking shears (if available)
Craft glue
Scraps of multicolored calico print fabric
Dark marker (or fabric paint in squeeze bottle)
Rickrack trim
Hole punch
Narrow ribbon or yarn
Small plastic hinged note clip
Small notepad (or sheets of paper stapled together)
Pencil or pen

INSTRUCTIONS:
1. Cut a large heart from cardboard. (If you want to make a miniature notepad holder, cut a smaller heart. You will need to use a tiny notepad and miniature pen or pencil.)
2. Cut square patches from fabric. Trim the edges with pinking shears for a decorative design. Cut out one heart-shaped patch.
3. Cover the cardboard heart with the fabric squares, overlapping the edges.
4. Glue the fabric in place.
5. Glue the heart-shaped patch on the fabric as shown.
6. After the glue dries, use a marker or fabric paint to write "Love one another" on the heart-shaped patch.
7. Glue rickrack trim around the edges.
8. Glue the note clip near the top of the heart. Let it dry.
9. Tie a piece of ribbon or yarn to the eraser end of a pencil or the unpointed end of a pen. Add a dab of glue to keep the yarn or ribbon from sliding off the pencil or pen.
10. Punch a hole in the top of the heart. Tie the other end of the ribbon or yarn through the hole.
11. Punch two more holes in the heart at the top on each side. Lace another piece of ribbon through the holes, and tie a bow so the heart can hang on the wall.
12. Clip the notepad to the note clip. (If you don't have a plastic note clip, glue the back of the notepad directly to the fabric.)
13. Write a message or a Bible verse about love on the notepad.

OTHER IDEA:
- Cover the heart with clear adhesive plastic to protect it. Then glue the rickrack trim over the plastic.

TEDDY BEAR CARD

"Greet one another with . . . love." 1 Peter 5:14a

MATERIALS:
Patterns (pages 23-24)
Pastel paper
Glue stick
Scissors
Crayons, markers, or colored pencils
Decorative trims (glitter glue, heart stickers, etc.)

INSTRUCTIONS:
1. Make a copy of the patterns on pages 23-24. Copy them on pastel paper. If possible, use a two-sided copy machine so the patterns can be copied on the front and back of a single sheet of paper, or reproduce the patterns on separate sheets of paper and cut them out. Glue the sheets together back-to-back to make a greeting card. (To avoid bubbles, use a glue stick instead of regular glue.)
2. Trim the edges, and throw away the excess.
3. Fold the card along the broken line in the middle.
4. Fold down on the V-shape; then open the card.
5. Reverse the direction of the vertical fold in the top V-section by pushing it to the inside.
6. Holding the folded side of the card with one hand, pinch the pop-up portion on the inside and pull down. As you pull down and press, the card will fold properly.
7. Color the pictures on the inside and outside of the card.
8. Decorate the card with items such as glitter glue and heart stickers.
9. Sign your name on the blank line on the inside of the card. Write on the appropriate blank lines on the outside your name and the person to whom you will send the card.

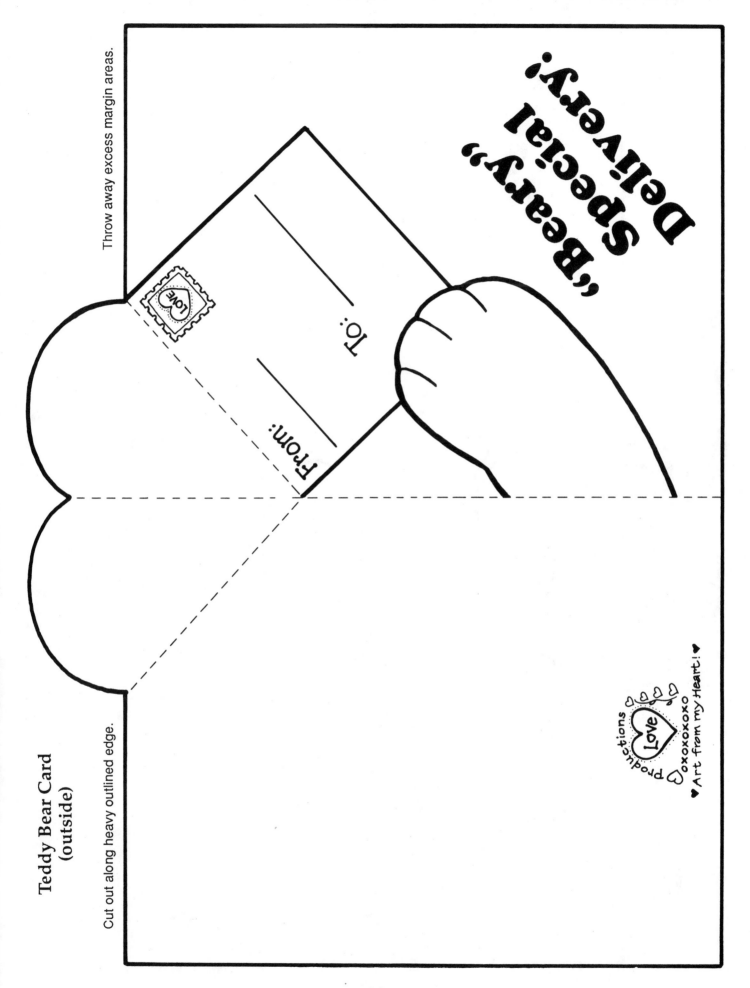

VALENTINE PUZZLE CARD

"For God so loved the world that he gave his one and only Son, that whoever believes in him shall not perish but have eternal life." John 3:16

MATERIALS:
Colored poster board or lightweight white cardboard
Pencil
Sharp scissors or hobby knife
Fine-line markers
Stamped envelope

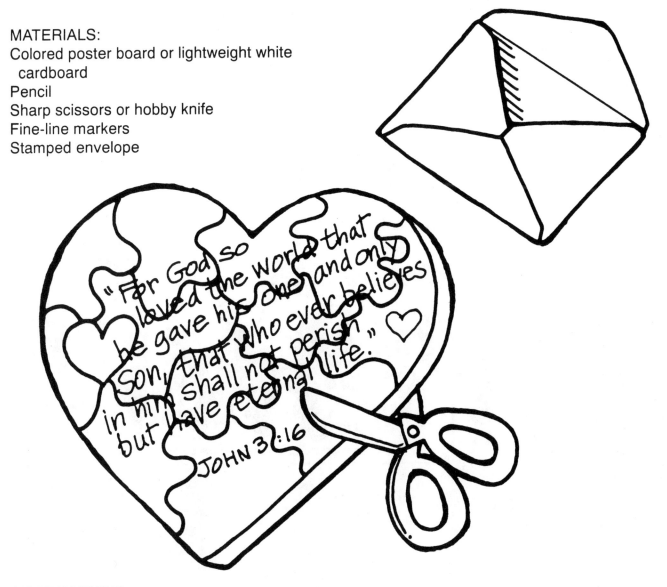

INSTRUCTIONS:
1. Draw and cut out a large heart from poster board or cardboard.
2. Using a pencil, write on the heart a Bible verse about love, such as John 3:16. Trace over the words with a dark marker. Sign your name, and write a personal message on the back. Let the ink dry.
3. Using a pencil, sketch curved lines to outline puzzle pieces as shown. Draw at least five pieces but not so many that they become too small and flimsy. You may want to make one of the puzzle pieces a heart shape.
4. Ask an adult to help you cut out the pieces, especially if you're using a sharp hobby knife.
5. Put the puzzle pieces in an envelope. Seal it shut, and send it to a friend or relative. Write a message on the back of the sealed envelope telling the person to "have fun" putting the puzzle together to discover the valentine message!

PALM SUNDAY PUPPET SHOE BOX STAGE

"They took palm branches and went out to meet him, shouting, 'Hosanna!'. . . Jesus found a young donkey and sat upon it."   John 12:13a, 14a

MATERIALS:
Palm Sunday puppet patterns (page 27)
Large shoe box
Construction paper
Hobby knife
Scissors
Crayons or markers
Tongue depressors or wooden craft sticks
Transparent tape
Glue
Clear adhesive plastic

INSTRUCTIONS:
1. Remove the shoe box lid. Turn the shoe box on its side to make a stage.
2. Cover the inside and outside of the shoe box with construction paper.
3. Decorate the inside to look like Bible-time scenery with a palm tree, sun, clouds, etc.
4. Make copies of the puppet patterns on page 27.
5. Color the patterns, and cover them with clear adhesive plastic.
6. Glue a wooden craft stick or tongue depressor to the back of each pattern to create a stick puppet. You may prefer to tape the puppets to the back of the box as scenery pieces which won't move, rather than using them as puppets.
7. Ask an adult to cut a slit wide enough and long enough along the bottom of the box so the stick attached to the Jesus puppet can be moved in the slit. If the other figures are to be movable puppets, make slit tracks in the back of the box in which to move them too.
8. Move the puppet back and forth in the slit to act out the story of Jesus entering Jerusalem on Palm Sunday.

Jesus

People

CROSS SILHOUETTE PAINTING

"You are looking for Jesus the Nazarene, who was crucified. He has risen!" — Mark 16:6a

MATERIALS:
White or light-colored construction or water-
  color paper
Pencil
Watercolor paints
Paintbrushes
Container of water
Paper towels
Wide black marker, black poster paint, or
  india ink
Fine-line black pen
Glue
Scissors
Black construction paper
Black yarn or string
Clear tape

INSTRUCTIONS:
1. On the sheet of white or light-colored paper, lightly sketch crosses on a hill, making the center cross the largest.
2. Paint a beautiful sunrise in back of the crosses. Brush a small amount of water on the paper; then dab on and brush horizontal streaks of orange, yellow, red, and purple paint. The colors will blend into lovely shades that look like a sunrise.
3. Blot the painting with paper towels to soak up excess water so the colors don't get "muddy" looking.
4. Leave an area on the hill unpainted where you can later write a Bible verse.
5. Use wide black pen, black paint, or india ink to make solid silhouettes of the crosses and the hill. The dark silhouettes will stand out against the beautiful sky.
6. After the painting dries, use a fine-line black pen to write the words "He has risen!" or the Bible verse from Mark 16:6a as shown.
7. Glue the painting to a sheet of black construction paper which is larger than the painting. Trim the edges as needed to make a frame.
8. Fold the black paper forward and crease it along the edges of the painting to make a three-dimensional "shadow box" frame. Pinch and crease the frame to make diagonal corners.
9. Cut a piece of black yarn or string, and tape it to the back of the frame near the top. Hang the painting on a wall.

"STAINED GLASS WINDOW" AND CROSS MAGNET

"Christ will suffer and rise from the dead . . . and repentance and forgiveness of sins will be preached in his name." Luke 24:46b, 47a

MATERIALS:
Sturdy cardboard or poster board scraps
Black construction paper
Multicolored felt scraps
Scissors
Craft glue
Black marker
Magnets or magnetic tape

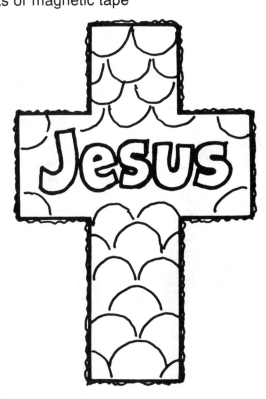

INSTRUCTIONS:
1. Cut cardboard or poster board into a small cross or church window shape.
2. Cover the shape with black paper.
3. Cut small teardrop-shaped pieces from felt. Layer and glue the pieces of felt on black paper to look like stained glass. Let some of the black background show through if you want it to look like a leaded window frame.
4. Use a black marker or cut letters from black felt, and glue them on the "stained glass" to share a message. The words may be "He is alive!" or the name "Jesus."
5. Attach a magnet or a strip of magnetic tape to the back.
6. Hang the window or cross on a refrigerator door or a metal file cabinet. You may wish to use the magnet to post slips of paper with Bible verses on them during the Easter season.

PRESSED FLOWERS EASTER BOOKMARK

"He has risen from the dead." Matthew 28:7a

MATERIALS:
Lightweight tagboard or heavy paper
Scissors
Tiny flowers (fresh or predried)
Typing paper
Several heavy books
Tweezers
Craft glue
Marker
Clear adhesive plastic
Hole punch
Yarn, ribbon, or premade bookmark tassel

INSTRUCTIONS:
1. For this project, use tiny flowers that have already been dried or dry tiny fresh flowers from a garden.
2. To dry flowers, place them between folded sheets of typing paper. Place the paper inside the pages of a heavy book. Put several other heavy books on top to press the flowers. Let fresh flowers dry thoroughly, probably several weeks.
3. Cut a small cross from tagboard or heavy paper.
4. Use tweezers to arrange the dried flowers on the cross. Put a tiny dab of glue behind each flower to keep it in place.
5. Write "Happy Easter!" on the cross.
6. After it is completely dry, cover the cross with clear adhesive plastic. Trim the edges.
7. Punch a hole at the top of the cross.
8. Insert a premade tassel into the hole, or make a tassel from yarn. You may prefer to tie a pretty ribbon through the hole.
9. Give or send this bookmark to someone, or use it in your Bible to mark the story of Christ's death and resurrection.

"STAINED GLASS WINDOW" COOKIES

"He [Jesus] said, 'I am the light of the world.'"   John 8:12b

MATERIALS:
Lollipops or hard candies (variety of transparent colors)
Sugar cookie dough (your favorite recipe or premade, frozen dough)
Hammer or rolling pin
Dull knife
Aluminum foil
Cookie sheet
Nonstick baking spray
Regular oven or toaster oven
Kitchen timer or wristwatch

INSTRUCTIONS:
1. Crumble candy and lollipops into small chunks. To do this, wrap each color of candy in a piece of foil, leaving the wrappers on. With an adult's help, use a hammer or rolling pin to crush the candy. Set aside the separate colors for later use.
2. Cover a cookie sheet with a clean sheet of foil. Spray the foil lightly with nonstick spray.
3. Slice the dough into small pieces and roll them in your hand until they become soft and pliable.
4. Mold the dough in the shape of a church window with a peaked top as shown. Poke open spaces where candy will be added later. (Remember that the dough will puff up when baked and the open spaces in the cookie will become smaller.)
5. Unwrap and sprinkle the crumbled candy into the empty spaces on the cookie to make the "stained glass." Sprinkle only one color in each space.
6. Bake the cookies at 375 degrees for 8 to 10 minutes. Toaster ovens get hotter quicker, so lower the temperature if needed. The outside of the baked window should be light brown but firm, and the crumbled candy should melt into a smooth, glass-like surface.
7. Let the cookie cool and harden. When you hold the cookie up to a lamp or the sun, the light will shine through the colored panes.
8. Enjoy eating the cookie, or give it to someone as an Easter gift.

OTHER IDEAS:
- Experiment by making windows in a variety of shapes and sizes.
- Wrap cookies in colored plastic wrap. Make tiny cards with Bible verses or Easter greetings on them. Attach the cards to wrapped cookies to make gifts.

EASTER PLANT-PICK DECORATION

"After his suffering, he [Jesus] showed himself . . . and gave many convincing proofs that he was alive."
                                                                                              Acts 1:3a

MATERIALS:
Self-hardening clay
Bamboo skewer
Toothpick

INSTRUCTIONS:
1. Use clay to mold an Easter symbol, such as a butterfly or a flower. If you're making a cross, you may wish to braid soft clay to make the vertical and horizontal pieces. Then press and rub the two pieces together to make the cross shape.
2. Push a bamboo skewer through the center of the clay symbol.
3. Use a toothpick to engrave words on the clay–"Jesus lives!" or "Happy Easter!"
4. After the clay dries and hardens, give the plant-pick to someone. Explain that it is a decoration to stick in a planter or a flowerpot.

OTHER IDEAS:
- Make the plant-pick from other types of self-hardening clay, such as colorful craft molding plastic or clay that you make from flour, water, salt, and oil.
- You may wish to paint the clay symbol and shellac it with protective varnish.
- Decorate a large Styrofoam™ cup using crayons and Easter stickers. Plant some grass seed or flowers in the cup, and stick the plant-pick in it.
- If your container is not very tall or heavy, such as a Styrofoam™ cup, break the bamboo stick off so the container won't topple over.

EASTER "SON"RISE FLOWERPOT

"They came and told us that they had seen a vision of angels, who said he [Jesus] was alive."
Luke 24:23b

MATERIALS:
Terra-cotta (brown clay) or plastic flowerpot and matching water dish
Acrylic paints
Small paintbrushes
Small flowering plants or seeds
Potting soil
Water container

INSTRUCTIONS:
1. Paint a clay or plastic pot and water dish with a spring design, such as flowers, a sun, or butterflies. Then paint these words on it: "Jesus Is Alive!"
2. After the paint dries, fill the pot with potting soil, and plant seeds or a small flowering plant.
3. Water the seeds or the plant.
4. Put the plant on your family's table so they will see it at breakfast on Easter morning. Remind them that Jesus, the Son of God, has risen and is alive! You may prefer to deliver the plant to someone who is ill. As the person watches the plant grow, he or she will be reminded that Jesus is alive!

OTHER IDEAS:
- Give this plant to someone, perhaps your pastor's family, at an Easter sunrise worship service.
- Deliver this plant to someone who is ill or lonely. Call it a "sunshine gift" to brighten the person's day. As the person watches the plant grow, he or she will be reminded that Jesus is alive.

EASTER "SON"RISE MOBILE

"We have seen his glory, the glory of the One and Only."   John 1:14b

MATERIALS:
Patterns (pages 35-36)
Scissors
Glue
Poster board or old manila folder
Crayons or markers
Clear adhesive plastic
Decorative materials (colored yarn, glitter paint pens, cotton balls)
Hole punch
String or yarn

INSTRUCTIONS:
1. Copy the cloud patterns on pages 35-36.
2. Color the sun, rainbow, and birds on the clouds.
3. Cut out and glue the clouds on poster board or an old manila folder to make the pieces sturdier.
4. Cover the clouds with clear adhesive plastic, and trim the edges.
5. Glue bits of cotton on the clouds and colored yarn on the bands of the rainbow. Be careful not to cover the words on the clouds. Outline the clouds and the sun with glitter, if desired.
6. Punch holes where indicated. Tie yarn or string through the holes to attach the clouds together to make a mobile as shown.
7. Hang the mobile from the ceiling to display during the Easter season.

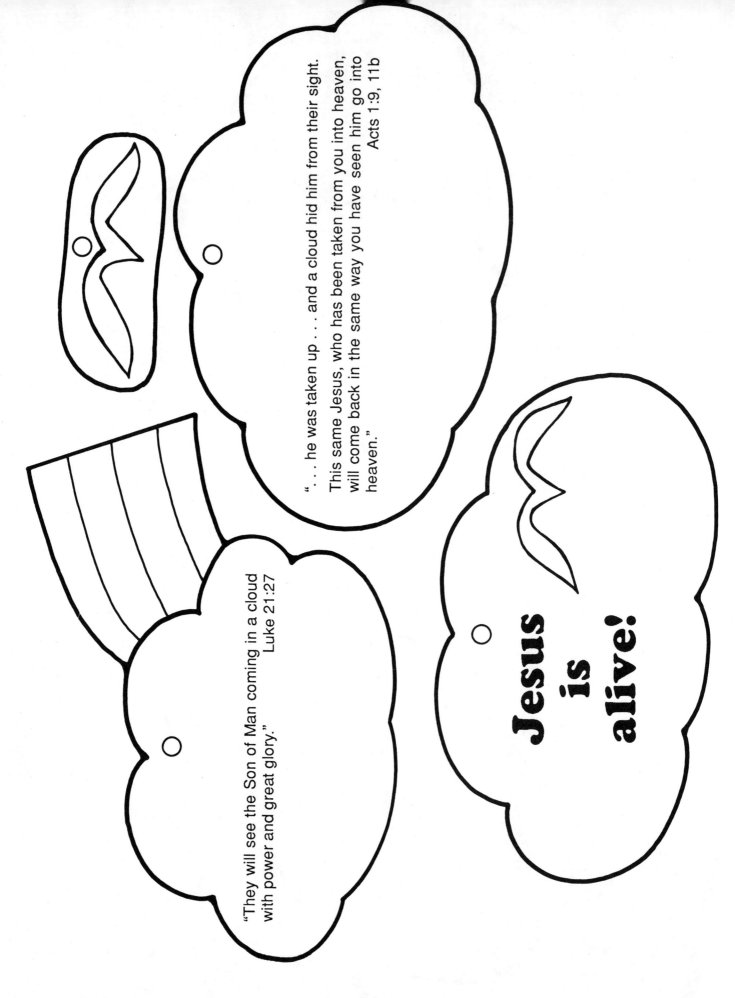

CRAYON BATIK EASTER WIND SOCK

"Let us rejoice and be glad and give him glory!" Revelations 19:7a

MATERIALS:
Muslin fabric (12" x 20")
Scissors
Chenille wire pipe cleaner (12" long)
Wax crayons
Iron and ironing board
Sheets of newspaper
Craft glue
Hole punch
Yarn or string

INSTRUCTIONS:
1. Snip parallel vertical lines along fabric to create fringe appoximately 10" long and 1½" wide.
2. Using crayons, draw a spring design of flowers on the top of the fabric. On the picture and fringe, write joyful phrases, such as "Rejoice!," "Happy Easter!," "Jesus Lives!," and "Hallelujah!"
3. Place the fabric between folded sheets of newspaper. Set an iron on a low temperature. With an adult's help, iron over the newspaper, using fresh sheets of newspaper as the crayon wax design soaks through. When the design shows through slightly on the back side of the fabric, the crayon design has absorbed and is set.
4. To make a hoop around the top edge, bend a chenille wire (pipe cleaner) into a round shape, and twist the ends together.
5. Fold the top edge of the fabric over the hoop, and glue it on the inside.
6. Glue the fabric along the back edges to form a tube shape. Press and hold the glued edges until they begin to dry, overlapping the fabric slightly to avoid a gap.
7. Use a hole punch to make two holes opposite each other in the fabric.
8. Lace yarn through the holes, and tie the ends together to hang up the wind sock.
9. Hang the wind sock outside on a nice (but not rainy) spring day so it flutters in the breeze.

HELPFUL HINTS:
- To keep the fabric from fraying, an adult can help hem the edges on a sewing machine.
- Buy antifray solution to spread on the edges of the fabric. The solution comes in a plastic squeeze bottle and hardens (somewhat like clear nail polish) as it dries.

EASTER BUTTERFLY MOBILE OR CARD

Have you ever seen a beautiful butterfly break out of its cocoon, then fly away? The butterfly reminds us that Jesus Christ rose from the grave so that we can live with Him forever!

MATERIALS:
Butterfly pattern (page 39)
Crayons or markers
Scissors
Clear adhesive plastic
Hole punch
Yarn or string

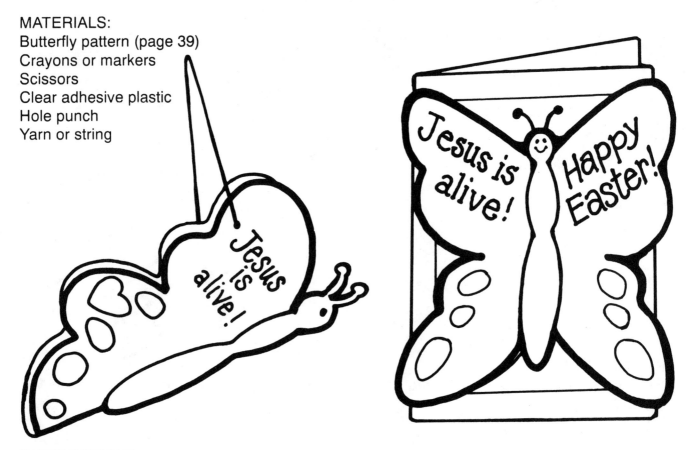

INSTRUCTIONS:
1. Copy the butterfly pattern on page 39.
2. Color the butterfly and cut it out.
3. Cover the butterfly with clear adhesive plastic. Trim the edges.
4. Fold the butterfly down the center, and crease the fold.
5. Punch two holes, where indicated, on the wings.
6. Lace and tie yarn or string through the holes to hang up the butterfly as an Easter decoration.

OTHER IDEAS:
- Decorate the wings with glitter paint, or use a cotton-tipped swab to make colorful poster-paint dots on the wings. Paint dots on half of the blank back side of the wings; then fold the wings closed. Press gently, and then unfold the wings to see the same design appear on the opposite half.
- Use the pattern to cut other butterflies from paper plates. Hang them from the ceiling to make a display.
- Tape a butterfly to the front of a folded sheet of construction paper to decorate an Easter card.

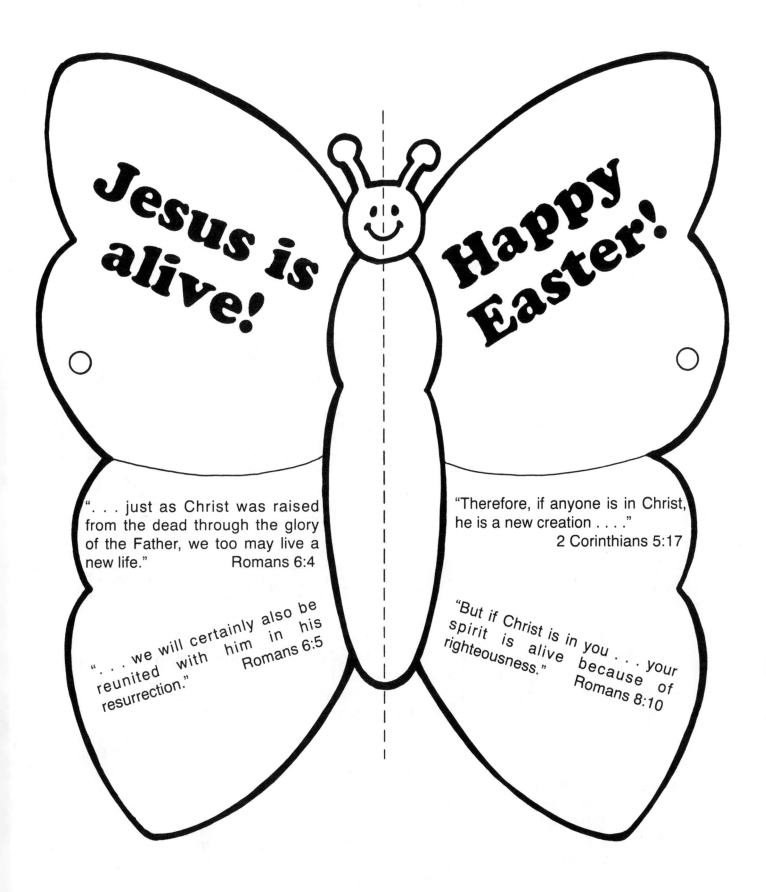

MOTHER'S BULLETIN BOARD

"Your love has given me great joy and encouragement."   Philemon 1:7a

MATERIALS:
Sturdy cardboard
Old wooden frame
Scissors
Felt, fabric, or burlap
Craft paint in squeeze bottles or permanent markers
Pom-poms
Tiny wiggle eyes
Yarn
Craft glue

INSTRUCTIONS:
1. Cut a piece of cardboard to fit your frame. (The cardboard must be sturdy but thin enough to slide into the frame even after it is covered with felt or fabric.)
2. Cover the cardboard with felt, fabric, or burlap and glue it down. Let it dry.
3. Slide the covered cardboard into the frame to make a bulletin board.
4. Cut letters from felt to spell "Mom's Memos!" Glue them near the top of the board.
5. Decorate the frame with springtime decorations, such as tiny birds, flowers, ladybugs, or fruit. Make these items from felt scraps and pom-poms. Glue tiny wiggle eyes on the animals. Use yarn for flower stems and other details.
6. Use paint or markers to add other decorations and words—"Mothers are a blessing!" "Joy," "Love," and "Peace."
7. If the frame doesn't already have a hanger, make one from sturdy yarn.
8. Post some notes on the board to remind your mother that you love and appreciate her. Give this gift to her to hang at home or in her office.

PENCIL OR KITCHEN UTENSIL HOLDER

A good mother provides food for her family and sets about her work vigorously.

See Proverbs 31:15, 17

MATERIALS:
Fabric, felt, colored adhesive plastic, or construction paper
Small or medium-sized empty cans or round containers without sharp edges
Scissors
Craft glue
Markers or fabric paint pens
Decorative trims (pom-poms, narrow ribbon, rickrack, etc.)

INSTRUCTIONS:
1. Cut a rectangular piece of fabric, felt, adhesive plastic, or construction paper to fit a round container, and glue it on.
2. Decorate with trims. For example, glue ribbon or rickrack around the top and bottom rims of the container. Make flowers and other designs by gluing on pom-poms and scraps of felt. Let the project dry.
3. Use markers or fabric paint pens to add a message, such as "Jesus loves my mom!"
4. Give the container to your mother. A small container, such as one made from a soup can, may be used for a pencil holder at home or at the office. A large container may be used to hold kitchen utensils or other tools your mother might use in her work.

OTHER IDEA:
- Cover small boxes and containers with matching fabric to make a desk set, including items such as note holder, paper clip holder, and computer diskette container. Give them to your mother to use at home or at the office.

"FRUIT OF THE SPIRIT" RECIPE BOX AND CARDS

"But the fruit of the Spirit is love, joy, peace, patience, kindness, goodness, faithfulness, gentleness and self-control."
                                                                      Galatians 5:22-23a

MATERIALS:
Small box with lid (to hold 3" x 5" cards)
Construction paper, plain-colored wrapping paper, or colored adhesive plastic
Scissors
Glue
Transparent tape
Decorative stickers (flowers, fruits, etc.) or pictures from greeting cards
Ink stamps and stamp pad
Fine-line markers or calligraphy pens
Lined 3" x 5" index or recipe cards
Old manila folders
Clear adhesive plastic

INSTRUCTIONS:
1. Cover the box and lid with colored paper.
2. Tape the lid loosely to the box so it will open and close.
3. On the outside of the box, print "Mom's Recipe Box." Also list the nine "fruits of the Spirit" found in Galatians 5:22-23a: love, joy, peace, patience, etc. (These are characteristics that God helps mothers show to their children!)
4. Decorate the box with stickers and ink stamps.
5. On some recipe cards write Bible verses, such as Galatians 5:22-23a, or others which describe your mom and ways she shows her love toward you and others.
6. On other cards you may wish to write short poems or messages to your mom.
7. You may want to write a "recipe" describing your mother's love to put in the box. Mix together:
       1 cup cheerfulness
     10 cups patience
       3 cups joy
       1 teaspoon tenderness, etc.
8. Cut category dividers from old manila folders. (You may want to ask an adult to help you do this.) An adult can probably provide you with old folders and show you how to set up a staggered filing system so it's easy to see all the labels at one time. Label the dividers with food categories–breads, casseroles, salads, desserts, etc.
9. Cover the box and the divider cards with clear adhesive plastic to protect them.
10. Label blank cards at the top to personalize them with your mother's name ("From Marcia's Kitchen"). Put the recipe cards in the box so your mother can write her favorite recipes on them. Mix your surprise messages in with these cards.
11. You may also want to include favorite recipes from a relative or neighbor.
12. Surprise your mother with this gift that she can use every day.

"COUNTRY CHARM" MOBILE

God gives mothers to all living creatures! Thank you, Lord, for mothers!

MATERIALS:
Patterns (pages 44-45)
Scissors
Glue
Lightweight cardboard or poster board
Crayons, markers, or colored pencils
Clear adhesive plastic
Hole punch
Yarn or string
Transparent tape

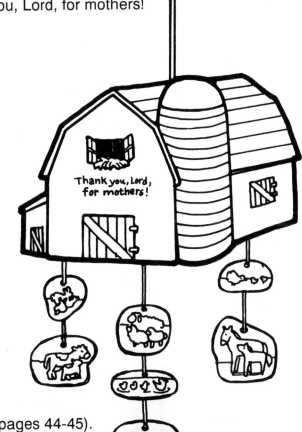

INSTRUCTIONS:
1. Make copies of the barn and animal patterns (pages 44-45).
2. Color the copies.
3. Glue the barn and animals on cardboard or poster board.
4. Cut out the barn and animals around the heavy outlines.
5. Write a short message to your mother or a favorite Bible verse on the back of the barn.
6. Cover the pieces with clear adhesive plastic. Trim the edges.
7. Punch holes on the pieces where indicated.
8. Cut yarn or string to desired lengths, and attach animals so they hang below the barn. You may tape or tie two sets of animals to one string, if you want.
9. Tie yarn or string through the hole at the top so your mother can hang up the mobile.

HELPFUL HINTS AND OTHER IDEAS:
- Instead of punching holes, you may prefer to tape yarn or string to the back of the pieces.
- You may wish to reproduce the patterns on colored paper, for example, the barn on red and the animals on light brown.
- If you want to make a smaller mobile, use a copy machine which can reduce the size of the patterns.
- Use the patterns for other creative projects—greeting cards, murals, posters, etc.
- Experiment with other materials to make the mobile, such as self-hardening clay and animal cookie cutters, shrink plastic (to make miniature figures), or molding clay. Make sure an adult helps you if the directions require you to bake the pieces in an oven.
- Just for fun, go somewhere, such as a farm or zoo, with your mother to see some real baby animals with their mothers!

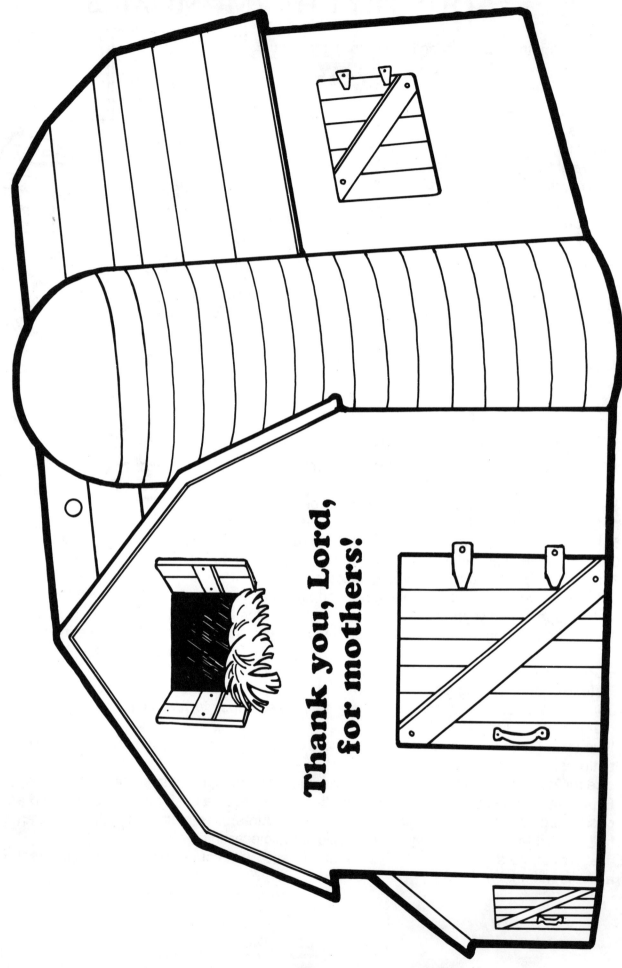

MOM'S "TREAT" JAR

"How sweet are your words to my taste, sweeter than honey to my mouth!" Psalm 119:103

MATERIALS:
Lightweight cotton fabric
Cotton batting (stuffing)
Scissors or pinking shears
Craft glue
Narrow ribbon
White paper and transparent tape or white adhesive jar labels
Medium-sized plastic or glass jar with lid
Fine-line pen
Decorative trims (tiny strawflowers, ribbon rosettes, etc.)
Treats (small candies, trail mix, etc.)

INSTRUCTIONS:
1. Cut a circle of fabric to cover the jar's lid and overlap the lid's edge by approximately 1" to 2", depending on the size of the jar. Use pinking shears to make a decorative edge that won't unravel easily.
2. Glue a bit of cotton batting on the lid under the fabric, or glue the fabric directly to the lid. (Secure the fabric to the lid with a metal jelly jar ring, if you're using that type of jar.)
3. Tie and glue ribbon around the fabric or on the jar ring to keep it in place. Let it dry.
4. Add decorative trim, such as strawflowers, to the tied ribbon and bow.
5. Cut a label from white paper or use a premade label. Write a message on it, such as "God made a sweet treat when He created mothers!" or "You're sweeter than honey (or sugar), Mom!" Later fill the jar with real honey or wrapped honey-flavored candies or sugar. Include a card with Psalm 119:103 written on it and give it to your mom.

POTPOURRI SACHET

"And the house was filled with the fragrance of the perfume." John 12:3c

MATERIALS:
Lightweight cotton fabric or fine-mesh nylon net
Scissors and pinking shears
Yarn or narrow ribbon
Premade potpourri or cologne and cotton ball
Hole punch
Paper scrap
Pen
Decorations (tiny dried flowers, ribbon rosettes, etc.)
Craft glue

INSTRUCTIONS:
1. Cut an 8" circle or square of fabric or nylon net.
2. Make a decorative edge with pinking shears.
3. Place some potpourri on the center of the fabric or nylon net, or dab a bit of cologne on a cotton ball and place in the center of the fabric.
4. Gather the fabric with your fingers near the top, and tie with yarn or ribbon to keep the potpourri or cotton ball inside.
5. Cut a tiny card from paper. Write a Mother's Day message on it, such as "God made mothers special!"
6. Punch a hole in the card, tie yarn or ribbon through it, and attach it to the sachet.
7. Glue decorations such as tiny flowers or ribbon rosettes to the fabric.
8. Your mother will enjoy putting this sachet in a drawer or on a shelf to make the area smell nice.

HELPFUL HINTS:
- Make your own potpourri from nutmeg, cinnamon, and other sweet-smelling spices, or collect natural items such as dried rose petals, dried weeds and dab them with floral or fruit-scented potpourri oils which you may purchase at craft stores. Ask at craft stores for ideas or books with recipes describing how to make your own potpourri.
- If you're using nylon net, make sure that it is finely woven mesh and that the potpourri mixture is thick enough not to leak through.

LACE DOILY BASKET

"Honor . . . your mother." Exodus 20:12a

MATERIALS:
Lightweight fabric or small fabric lace doily
Scissors and pinking shears
Fabric stiffener liquid (from fabric or craft shops)
Glass jar, plastic tumbler cup, or round spray can (with large, flat lid)
Waxed paper
Rubber band
Scrap of construction paper
Pen
Chenille wire (pipe cleaner)
Narrow fabric ribbon
Craft glue
Treats to fill basket (tiny flowers, candies, potpourri sachet, etc.)

INSTRUCTIONS:
1. Using scissors or pinking shears, cut a 6" circle of fabric, or use a fabric lace doily about that size.
2. Cut a circle from waxed paper the same size as the fabric or doily.
3. Soak the fabric or doily with fabric stiffener; then wring out the excess liquid.
4. Place the soaked fabric or doily on the waxed paper circle.
5. Turn the round object upside down. Mold the fabric or doily with the waxed paper around the bottom of the round object (waxed paper next to object). Secure it with a rubber band, allowing approximately 1" for a ruffle.
6. Allow the fabric to drip-dry overnight. Put extra waxed paper underneath to catch any drips. Gently pull and mold the edging away from the round object as the fabric or doily hardens, to make a ruffled edge.
7. After the fabric or doily dry, remove it from the round object. Tie a pretty ribbon around it.
8. Use a chenille wire, or a piece of narrow ribbon which has been stiffened with the fabric stiffener to make a handle for your new basket. Bend and glue the handle in place.
9. Make a tiny card from construction paper for your mother. Write a short poem or her favorite Bible verse on the inside of the card.
10. Fill the basket with a treat, such as tiny flowers, candy, or a potpourri sachet. (Make a sachet from fabric which matches your basket by following the directions on page 47.)
11. Surprise your mom with this gift on Mother's Day.

OTHER IDEA:
- Use two layers of fabric circles to make the basket. The inner layer might be a pretty floral print fabric, and the outer layer could be made from a delicate lace doily.

A SPECIAL MOM'S T-SHIRT

"Parents are the pride of their children." Proverbs 17:6b

MATERIALS:
Plain T-shirt (or sweatshirt) to fit your mother
Premade cardboard shirt frame (or cut one yourself)
Pencil or disappearing ink outline pen for fabric
Craft glue
Permanent fabric markers or fabric paint pens

INSTRUCTIONS:
1. Ask an adult (other than your mom!) to help you buy a shirt. (Wash to preshrink it before starting project.)
2. Stretch the shirt carefully, and slide it on a cardboard frame so that the shirt lies flat.
3. Use a pencil or disappearing ink fabric pen to lightly sketch a simple drawing of you and your mother on the front of the shirt.
4. Write words such as "God made my mom special!"
5. Paint the picture, and go over the words with the fabric markers or pens. Let the paint dry.
6. Give your mother this T-shirt. When she wears it, everyone will see that she's special and that you are proud of her!

MOM'S FRAMED MIRROR

Do you see Jesus in your mother's life? Give her this gift and tell her how much her good example means to you.

MATERIALS:
Square mirror tile (7" x 7")
Cotton fabric (12" x 12")
Sturdy corrugated cardboard (10" x 10")
Right angle square tool or straight-edge ruler
Pencil
Scissors or hobby knife
Craft glue
Cotton batting (10" x 10")
Straight pins
Fabric pen, fabric paint pen, or regular marker
Prepainted wooden heart or heart cut from colored poster board or cardboard
Decorative trims (narrow ribbon, cotton eyelet lace, etc.)
Chenille wire (pipe cleaner)
Poster board or manila folder
Crayons or markers

INSTRUCTIONS:
1. Ask an adult to cut a cardboard frame for you. The outside edge of the frame should be about 10" x 10". The inside edges along the center opening should be about 5" x 5". The person who cuts it out should draw pencil lines, using a ruler or a right angle square tool. The center piece should be cut out and saved for another project. The sides of the frame should be about 2½" wide.
2. Cut the fabric about 1" larger than the frame on all sides.
3. Cut a piece of cotton batting the exact size of the frame. Glue it on the frame.
4. Glue the back of the fabric to the cotton batting.
5. Pull the overlapping outside edges of the fabric behind the frame. Be careful not to pull so tightly that the cardboard bends. Fold and clip the corners as needed so that the overlapping edges of the fabric can be pulled behind without causing puckered corners. Glue the fabric edges behind the frame. Use straight pins to keep the fabric in place while it dries.
6. Ask an adult to cut an X-shape in the center of the fabric which is stretched over the frame. Stop cutting approximately ⅛" before reaching the cardboard frame, so the batting won't show later.
7. There should be four triangular fabric pieces in the center of the frame. Pull each piece to the back of the frame and glue. Use straight pins to hold the fabric in place.

8. When the glue is dry, remove the straight pins.
9. Decorate the frame with ribbon, eyelet trim, etc.
10. On a wooden or cardboard heart, write "You reflect God's love!" Glue the heart to the frame.
11. Glue the mirror tile behind the frame and let it dry.
12. Bend the ends of a chenille wire to make small right angles so it won't slip off when glued. Bend the wire in the middle, and glue the bent ends to the back top of the frame to make a hanger.
13. Cut a piece of poster board or a piece from an old manila folder, and glue it to the back of the frame.
14. Draw a picture of your mother and you, or write a Bible verse on the back of the frame.
15. Your mother will appreciate using this mirror each day and being reminded that she is a reflection of God's love.

OTHER IDEA:
- Use a low-temperature glue gun to attach a sturdy brass ring to the back of the frame, rather than making the hanger from a chenille wire.

MOM'S TOTE BAG

"A mother comforts her child." Isaiah 66:13a

MATERIALS:
Pattern (page 53)
Plain canvas tote bag
Transfer paper used for fabric
Permanent fabric pens or paint pens
Sharpened pencil
Trims (wiggle eyes, ribbon, rickrack, pom-poms, etc.)
Scissors
Craft glue

INSTRUCTIONS:
1. Reproduce the bunny pattern on page 53.
2. Place the canvas bag flat on a smooth surface. Place the transfer paper on the bag and the pattern over it. Trace over the pattern to transfer it to the front of the bag.
3. Decorate the bunny design, and make borders on the bag by using fabric pens or paint pens. Let the bag dry.
4. Glue decorative trim such as ribbon or rickrack on the bag. You may wish to glue wiggle eyes on the bunnies and a pom-pom ball on the mother bunny's tail.
5. Your mother will enjoy using this bag to carry books, office items, mending and sewing projects, craft supplies, groceries, etc.

HELPFUL HINTS AND OTHER IDEAS:
- Purchase an inexpensive canvas tote bag, fabric transfer paper, paint pens, etc., at craft or fabric shops.
- Make matching T-shirts or sweatshirts for your mother and you, using the bunny pattern. Decorate the shirts and have fun wearing them when you go out together.
- If the canvas is lightweight enough for paint to soak through it, cut a piece of sturdy cardboard, and place it under the part of the bag you paint.

FLOWER POP-UP CARD

"Her children . . . call her blessed." Proverbs 31:28a

MATERIALS:
Patterns (page 55)
Construction paper (9" x 12")
Pastel colored paper
Scissors
Scrap of lightweight poster board or old manila folder
Glue
Crayons or markers
Transparent tape

INSTRUCTIONS:
1. Copy the flower and flowerpot on page 55, preferably on pastel paper.
2. Color the flower and pot and cut them out.
3. Glue the flower and the stem to a scrap of poster board or an old manila folder, and trim the edges.
4. Cut a slit at the bottom of the stem where indicated.
5. Cut a slit on the flowerpot where indicated. Tape along the sides of the slit on the back so the paper doesn't tear.
6. Slide the flower stem into the slit on the flowerpot.
7. Fold back the bottom of the flower stem on the broken lines. Tape the folded ends to the stem so the flower will not slide out of the pot.
8. Glue the flowerpot picture to the front of a folded sheet of construction paper to make a greeting card. (Do not glue down the flower, so it can slide up and down.)
9. Sign your name on the blank line on the flowerpot. Write a special message to your mother inside the card.
10. Your mother will enjoy pulling up the flower to watch it "grow" and to see the message on the stem. Tell her that your love for her is growing every day!

OTHER IDEAS:
- Decorate the picture with trims such as tiny ribbon bows or glitter glue.
- Rather than making a greeting card, glue the picture on a sheet of construction paper to make a framed picture for your mother to hang on a wall.

CRAYON BATIK HANDKERCHIEF

"He [the Lord] will turn the hearts of the fathers to their children, and the hearts of the children to their fathers."

Malachi 4:6a

MATERIALS:
Wax crayons
Plain white handkerchief
Masking tape
Iron and ironing board
Newspaper

INSTRUCTIONS:
1. Place the handkerchief on a table or flat surface, and tape it down to hold it flat.
2. Using crayons, draw a simple picture of your father and you on the handkerchief. Write a message, such as "I love my dad!" Sign your name and write the date in a corner. Remove the tape and throw it away.
3. Place the flattened handkerchief in a folded sheet of newspaper.
4. Set an iron on a low temperature. With an adult's help, iron over the newspaper, using fresh sheets of newspaper as the crayon wax absorbs into them. When the colored picture shows through on the back of the handkerchief, the design has permanently set into the fabric.
5. Your father will enjoy using this handkerchief because you decorated it!

COMPUTER FLOPPY DISK FILE

"Wise men store up knowledge."

Proverbs 10:14a

MATERIALS:
Computer pattern
Shoe box with lid
Construction paper or colored adhesive plastic
Glue
Transparent tape
Crayons and markers
Old manila folders
Scissors

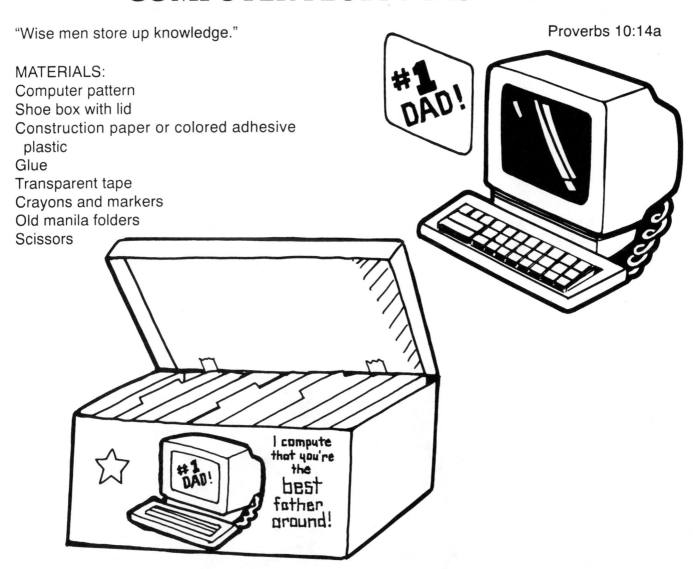

INSTRUCTIONS:
1. Cover the shoe box and lid with construction paper or colored adhesive plastic.
2. Copy the computer pattern above, color it, and cut it out.
3. Glue the computer to the outside of the box. Draw other pictures, if desired, using crayons or markers.
4. Write words such as "#1 Dad!" or "I compute that you're the best father around!" on the box.
5. Tape the lid to the box so it can be opened and closed easily.
6. Cut small box dividers from old manila folders which your father can label with his own categories.
7. Give this gift to your father. Explain that he can file and store computer disks and diskettes in it to use at work or home.

OTHER IDEA:
- If your father doesn't use a computer, decorate a box for him to file bank check receipts in or to store other items, such as tools or fishing gear.

DAD'S TV REMOTE CONTROL HOLDER

Do you ever tell your dad how much you appreciate him? Why not make him a useful gift to let him know you think he's a great guy?

MATERIALS:
Small rectangular box (big enough to hold a remote control)
Scissors
Construction paper, colored adhesive plastic, or felt
Glue or transparent tape
Sports patterns (page 59)
Decorative stickers of sports equipment or other hobbies
Crayons or markers

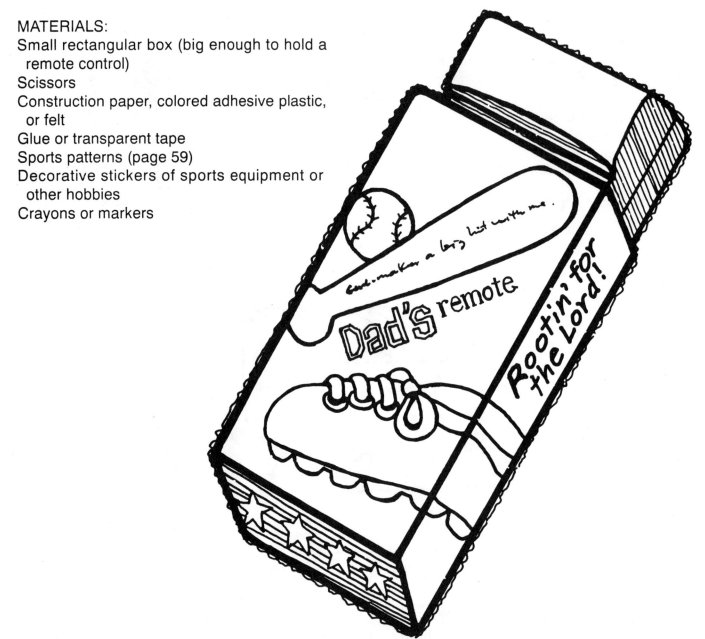

INSTRUCTIONS:
1. Cut off the top end of the box or the side if it's smaller.
2. Cover the box with paper, plastic, or felt.
3. Copy one or more of the sports equipment patterns on page 59. Choose ones that represent sports your father enjoys watching on television. Color and cut them out; then glue them to the outside of the box. (You may need to reduce the size of the patterns on a copy machine.) Draw other symbols, or attach stickers to represent your father's hobbies.
4. Write "Dad's remote" and "Rootin' for the Lord!" on the box.
5. Your father can keep the remote control in this box.

DAD'S NOTE CLIPS/BOOKMARKS

"Parents are the pride of their children." Proverbs 17:6b

MATERIALS:
Plastic note clips or large paper clips
Decorative stickers
Computer pattern (page 57) or sports patterns (page 59)
Scissors
Poster board scraps
Glue
Transparent tape
Markers
Clear adhesive plastic

INSTRUCTIONS:
1. Decorate large paper clips or plastic note clips with stickers, or reduce the patterns (pages 57 and 59) on a copy machine. Color the patterns and cut them out.
2. Glue the patterns or attach stickers to poster board scraps; then cover them with clear adhesive plastic to make them sturdier. Glue the patterns or stickers to large clips or plastic note clips.
3. Use a marker to write words such as "Dad's clip" on the clips.
4. Your father may use this gift as a bookmark or to hold a notepad or memo notes.

DAD'S SWEATSHIRT AND CAP

God tells us in His Word that fathers are very important. Does your dad know how important he is to you? Show him with this gift.

MATERIALS:
Sweatshirt and baseball cap to fit your father
Sport patterns (page 59)
Fabric transfer paper
Pencil
Fabric paint pens in squeeze bottles

INSTRUCTIONS:
1. Wash and preshrink the sweatshirt.
2. Copy and cut out the sports patterns you want to use (page 59).
3. Use fabric transfer paper to transfer the patterns to the front of the sweatshirt. Trace over the patterns on top of the paper.
4. Paint the patterns with fabric paint. Draw different pictures to represent hobbies if your father isn't interested in sports. Paint additional pictures and words, such as "My Dad's #1," on the shirt and cap.
5. Your father will enjoy wearing the shirt and cap to sporting events and other places.

SPORTS WATER BOTTLE

"Let us run with perseverance the race marked out for us." Hebrews 12:1b

MATERIALS:
Plain plastic sports water bottle
Permanent (waterproof) paint pens or craft paint in squeeze bottles
Sport patterns (page 59)
Pencil

INSTRUCTIONS:
1. Paint pictures and write encouraging words on a sports bottle for your father.
2. Make copies of the sport patterns on page 59 and trace around them.
3. Paint them and let dry.
4. Your father can fill this bottle with water, juice, or soft drinks. He will enjoy taking it along when he attends or participates in sporting events or other outside activities. It will remind him that both the Lord and you are "cheering" for him!

DAD'S CHEF OR CARPENTRY APRON

Help your dad be a witness for Jesus with this gift.

MATERIALS:
Plain canvas butcher-type apron (preferably with pockets)
Disappearing ink fabric pen or regular pencil
Fabric paint pens

INSTRUCTIONS:
1. Decorate a butcher's apron for your father to use while woodworking, gardening, backyard barbecuing, gourmet cooking, etc. Decorate the pockets to hold his tools while he works.
2. Use a pencil or a disappearing fabric ink pen to sketch a design and message, such as those shown.
3. Paint over the design; then let it dry.
4. Surprise your dad with this useful gift, and volunteer to help him with his projects. He will probably be pleased to share his hobbies with you.

HELPFUL HINT:
- Buy inexpensive aprons and the other suggested supplies at craft or fabric shops.

HAND-PAINTED "POWER" NECKTIE

"I can do everything through him [Christ] who gives me strength."   Philippians 4:13

MATERIALS:
Solid-colored, cotton-blend necktie
Fabric paint pens

INSTRUCTIONS:
1. Ask an adult to help you find an inexpensive necktie to decorate, perhaps at a used clothing store. (Don't take one from your dad's closet!)
2. Use paint pens to decorate the tie with words, such as "Super Dad" or "God loves my dad, and so do I!" Let the paint dry.
3. When you give the tie to your dad, tell him it's a "power" tie and that you're glad his power to be a "super dad" comes from the Lord!

DAD'S TIE RACK

Here's a way to remind your dad every day that you love him!

MATERIALS:
Piece of sturdy wood (4" x 12", 1/2" thick) or
  premade wooden pegboard
Sandpaper
Three to four wooden pegs with screw-on
  metal backings
Acrylic paint
Paintbrushes
Two large brass curtain rings
Low-temperature glue gun and glue sticks

INSTRUCTIONS:
1. Ask an adult to help you cut a piece of wood to the desired size. Sand the edges until smooth, being careful not to get splinters in your fingers, or begin with a premade pegboard.
2. Screw wooden pegs into the board, spacing them evenly. (You may need an adult's assistance to do this.)
3. Paint the rack and let it dry. Paint a second coat if necessary to cover the wood totally. When the rack is dry, paint the words "Fathers are a gift from God!" on it.
4. Use a glue gun (with an adult's help) to attach brass rings to the back of the rack so your father can hang it up.
5. Your father can nail the rack to the wall or in a closet. He will appreciate being reminded how much you love him when he hangs his ties (and belts) on this rack.

DAD'S DECORATED COAT HANGER

This gift will help you encourage your dad every day by reminding him of God's love and yours.

MATERIALS:
12 feet of bump chenille wire (similar to fluffy, ridged pipe cleaners)
Wire coat hanger
Narrow decorative ribbon
Scissors
Decorative trim to represent hobbies (miniature sports equipment or sports patterns page 59)
Cardboard scraps
Hole punch
Markers
Clear adhesive plastic

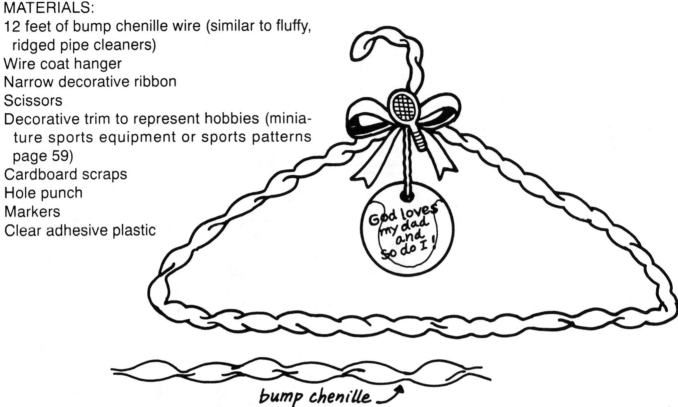

INSTRUCTIONS:
1. Wrap bump chenille around a hanger. Begin at the top and wrap chenille around until the hanger is entirely covered.
2. Tie a ribbon and decorative trim around the neck of the hanger as shown.
3. For the decorative trim, use a miniature symbol of your father's hobby, or draw a symbol on cardboard. Color and cut it out.
4. Add a special message to the hanger. For example, if you trimmed the hanger with a miniature tennis racket, cut a circle from cardboard and color it like a tennis ball. Write a phrase such as "What's the score?" or "God loves my dad and so do I!" on the ball. Cover it with clear adhesive plastic, punch a hole in it, and tie it with ribbon so it dangles in the center of the hanger.
5. Your father can use this hanger to hang up clothing or as a tie rack.

HELPFUL HINTS:
- Purchase bump chenille at craft stores. A long continuous piece of it is often sold in one package.
- Miniature sports equipment, such as tiny tennis rackets or baseball bats, can often be purchased at large craft or hobby shops.
- Use stickers of symbols to represent other hobbies, such as pianos, computers, or tools, and attach to cardboard.

FATHER'S DAY AWARD CERTIFICATE

"Honor your father." Exodus 20:12a

MATERIALS:
Award certificate (page 68)
Sport and/or computer patterns (pages 57 and 59)
Construction paper (9" x 12")
Glue
Scissors
Yarn
Transparent tape
Decorative stickers, rubber stamps and ink pad, magazine pictures (to represent activities your father likes)
Crayons or markers
Glitter pen
Wide blue ribbon

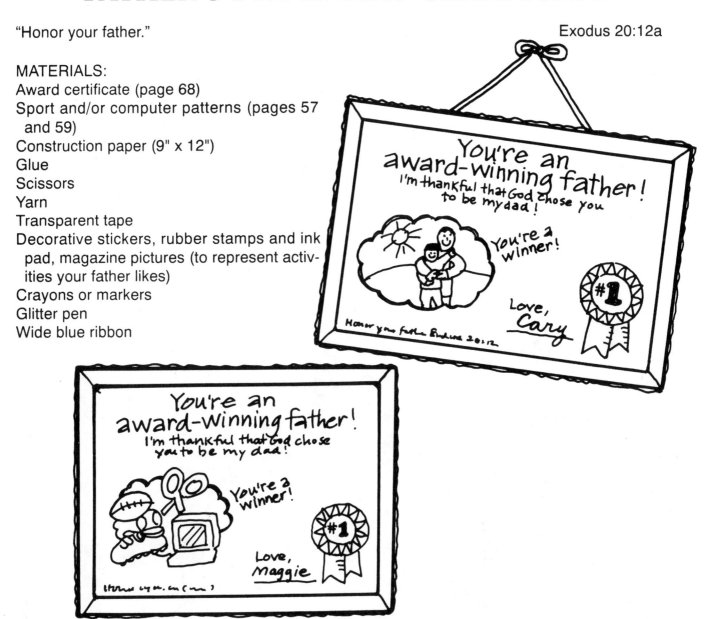

INSTRUCTIONS:
1. Copy the certificate on page 68. Trim and throw away the excess top edge.
2. Decorate the certificate to show your father's interests. For example, copy and color the computer and sports patterns, draw your own pictures, or cut pictures from magazines. Glue the pictures on the certificate.
3. You may also decorate the certificate with stickers or ink stamp designs. Outline the #1 circle with glitter to make it sparkle.
4. Glue blue ribbon to the award below the #1.
5. Sign your name on the blank line.
6. Glue the certificate to a sheet of construction paper to frame it. Tie yarn to the back so your father can hang it up to display.
7. You may want to plan a surprise Father's Day award ceremony with your family. Honor your dad by presenting this award certificate.

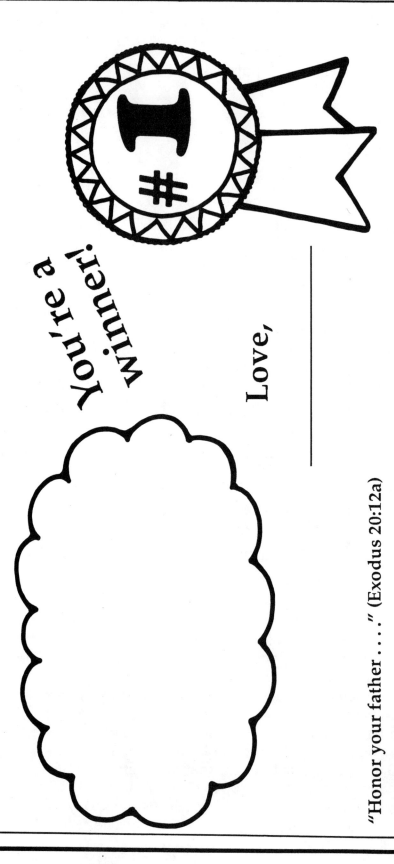

You're an award-winning father!

I'm thankful that God chose you to be *my* dad!

You're a #1 winner!

Love, _____

"Honor your father. . . ." (Exodus 20:12a)

⟵ (Cut off and remove excess margin.) ⟶

CLASS THANKSGIVING MURAL

"Let us come before him with Thanksgiving."   Psalm 95:2a

MATERIALS:
Mural (butcher) paper
Pencils
Crayons or markers
Instant camera and film
Scissors
Glue
Masking tape

INSTRUCTIONS:
* Note: These instructions are written for the adult who is working with a group of children.
 1. Cut a long piece of paper and tape it to a long table.
 2. Sketch and outline simple, large "bubble-type" letters that say "We give thanks!"
 3. Have students write words inside the letters, using markers or crayons. The words should begin with the letter in which they are written. The words should tell what they are thankful for. For example, inside the *w* they might write: wind, worship, water, whales, etc.
 4. Ask children to draw pictures of themselves on the mural. Adults may want to participate in this activity and draw self-portraits too.
 5. Label each self-portrait with the person's name.
 6. If you have an instant camera, take a close-up photograph of each person. Cut out the head of each person, and glue it to the self-portrait.
 7. Mount the mural on the wall or on a bulletin board in your classroom, or display it at your school office or church.

OTHER IDEA:
• You may also do this project at home with your family and other relatives as a Thanksgiving activity.

AUTUMN LEAVES WALL HANGING

God gives us autumn. See Jeremiah 5:24

MATERIALS:
Natural materials (dried weeds and leaves, seeds, etc.)
Thanksgiving and fall stickers or pictures cut from old greeting cards or gift wrap
Artificial silk-type fall leaves
Autumn-colored construction paper (9" x 12")
Scissors
Sturdy cardboard
Marker
Ruler
Clear adhesive plastic
Yarn or string
Tape
Glue

INSTRUCTIONS:
1. Begin with a sheet of autumn-colored construction paper.
2. Turn the sheet of paper to hang vertically.
3. Cut two strips of cardboard, approximately 1 1/2" wide and 10" long.
4. Cover the strips of cardboard with construction paper. Use a color which contrasts with the first piece of paper.
5. Tape or glue the cardboard strips to the top and bottom of the first sheet of paper.
6. Glue or tape flat items such as leaves, seeds, stickers, and pictures on the paper to make a fall collage. (You may want to go on a nature walk to gather some dried leaves and other materials.) Let the project dry.
7. Write on the top and bottom strips "Thanks, Lord, for this season!"
8. Cover the collage with clear adhesive plastic to protect and keep the items in place.
9. Tape yarn or string to the back to hang up, and display the collage during the Thanksgiving season.

THANKSGIVING PRAISE TREE

Let's be thankful and love God.

See Hebrews 12:28

MATERIALS:
Large dried tree branch with several offshoot branches
Plaster of paris and water
Large coffee can
Construction paper (fall colors)
Pencils
Scissors
Crayons or markers
Decorative stickers of things for which to be thankful
Hole punch
Yarn or string

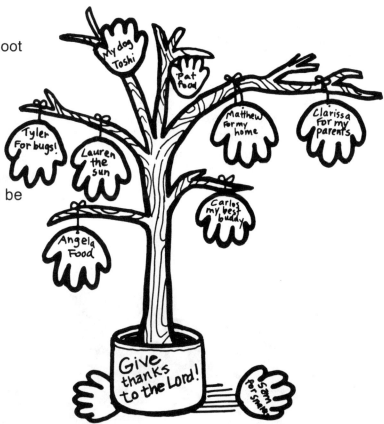

INSTRUCTIONS:
* Note: These instructions are written for the adult who is working with a group of children.
1. Trace around each child's hand on construction paper. (Use a variety of fall-colored paper: yellow, orange, tan, etc.) Cut out the hands.
2. Have each child write his name on his hand.
3. The child may draw a picture or write the name of something for which he is thankful. Instead of drawing the items, you may want to use stickers.
4. Brace a large branch in a weighted can so it doesn't topple over. Plaster of paris poured into the can works well for this purpose. (Add water to plaster powder, and follow directions provided with the plaster to mix it.)
5. Let the plaster dry thoroughly. Then cover the outside of the can with paper, and write on it "Give thanks to the Lord!"
6. Punch holes in the paper hands so they can hang from the tree like leaves.
7. Attach yarn or string through the holes, and hang the leaves on the tree branches. You may want to spread some of the leaves near the base of the tree as if they have fallen off.

OTHER IDEAS:
- You may want to do this project at home, using the tree for other seasonal holiday displays.
- Rather than making a three-dimensional display, make a bulletin board or wall display by cutting the tree trunk from brown construction paper or rolling and twisting brown paper from grocery bags to make a trunk shape.

THANKSGIVING MAGNETS

"There will be showers of blessing." Ezekiel 34:26b

MATERIALS:
Patterns from this page
Crayons or markers
Scissors
Craft glue
Lightweight cardboard
Clear adhesive plastic
Magnetic tape or small magnets

INSTRUCTIONS:
1. Copy the horn of plenty and squirrel patterns.
2. Color and cut them out.
3. Glue the figures to cardboard and trim the excess edges.
4. Cover the figures with clear adhesive plastic. Trim the edges.
5. Attach magnets or magnetic tape to the backs of the figures.
6. Use these magnets on a refrigerator or other metallic surface during the Thanksgiving season.

OTHER IDEAS:
- Glue bits of materials such as felt scraps on the figures to decorate them.
- Glue brown pom-poms on the squirrel's head and body and a scrap of brown fluffy chenille wire on his tail. Glue a tiny wiggle eye on the side of his head.

THANKSGIVING FELT BANNER

"Give thanks to the Lord." 1 Chronicles 16:8a

MATERIALS:
10" x 25" piece of autumn-colored felt
  (brown, gold, orange, etc.)
Scraps of felt in other autumn colors
Patterns on page 72
$1/4$" wooden dowel, 12" long
Markers
Scissors
Yarn or string
Two thumbtacks

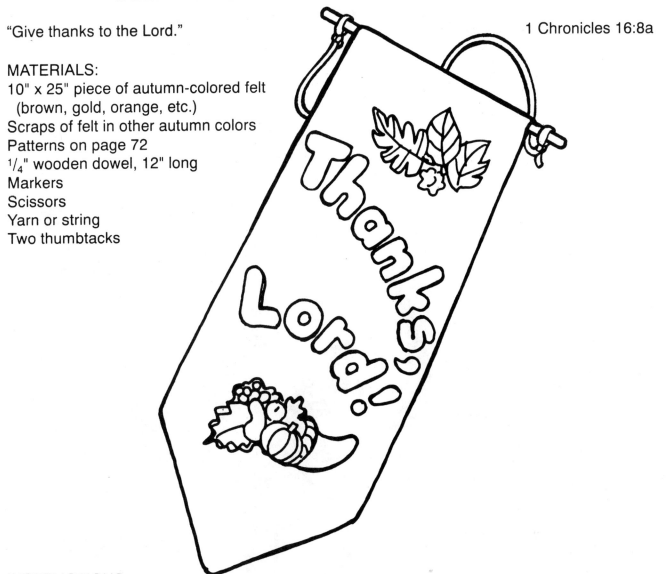

INSTRUCTIONS:
1. Holding the felt vertically, trim the bottom into a pointed edge as shown.
2. Cut letters from scraps of felt to spell words, such as "Thanks, Lord!" Glue them on the large felt piece.
3. Cut out felt decorations such as a turkey, cornucopia, or squirrel. You may wish to use the patterns on page 72. Enlarge or reduce the patterns as necessary. Outline the felt figures and draw details with markers. Glue the decorations on the banner.
4. Glue the top of the banner over the wooden dowel. Hold the overlapping felt firmly in place until it begins to dry.
5. Tie yarn or string to the dowel to hang the banner on a wall. Use thumbtacks to keep the yarn or string from sliding off the wooden dowel.

OTHER IDEA:
- Glue feathers on the turkey and brown pom-poms to its body to create a three-dimensional effect. Make its head and neck from a piece of brown chenille wire and glue on tiny wiggle eyes and a beak cut from a felt scrap.

MINIATURE HARVEST WREATH

A project that will remind us of harvest.

See Jeremiah 5:24

MATERIALS:
Sturdy cardboard
Scissors
Dried, natural items (nuts, seedpods, weeds acorns, etc.)
Craft glue
Autumn-colored narrow ribbon (gold, brown, orange, etc.)
Fine-line black or brown marker

INSTRUCTIONS:
1. Cut a piece of cardboard in a small ring, about 5" in diameter. The width of the ring from the center to the outside edge should be about 1".
2. Gather natural, dried materials and glue them on the ring. Let dry.
3. Wrap ribbon around the ring by weaving it over and under. Tie a small bow at the top.
4. Cut a cardboard circle to place behind the ring's center. Write on it "The Lord is good! So, thank Him!"
5. Glue the circle behind the decorated ring, making sure that the words show.
6. Hang the wreath on a wall or door.

OTHER IDEAS:
- Dab the wreath with potpourri liquid to make it smell nice.
- Go to a craft store and buy a small bag of potpourri mixture of prescented natural items. Then you won't need to gather other natural items.

THANKSGIVING FOOD SCULPTURES

"A generous man will himself be blessed, for he shares his food with the poor." Proverbs 22:9

MATERIALS:
Fruit (raisins, cherries, grapes, oranges, apples, etc.)
Vegetables (carrot and celery sticks, unbaked potatoes and yams, squash, cucumbers, leaf lettuce, parsley, etc.)
Tiny candies (chocolate chips, mints, etc.)
Marshmallows
Cloves
Toothpicks
Scraps of paper
Fine-line markers

INSTRUCTIONS:
1. Use firm fruits, vegetables, and marshmallows to make turkeys, people, etc.
2. Add details, such as eyes, by attaching dried cloves, small candies or raisins.
3. Attach body pieces together with toothpicks.
4. Carrot and celery sticks make interesting turkey tail feathers, arms, legs, etc. Lettuce and parsley make interesting hair on people sculptures. Add these types of vegetables just before displaying the projects, since they will dry out if exposed to the air for too long.
5. Make little paper signs with messages—"The Lord is good!" and "Happy Thanksgiving!" Attach these signs to the sculptures using toothpicks.
6. Use several food sculptures as a Thanksgiving centerpiece.
7. Make enough extra food sculptures to deliver some to hungry people, perhaps through a community food closet. You may prefer to deliver the sculptures and other foods to places where Thanksgiving dinner is served to needy people.

THANKSGIVING MINIATURE CENTERPIECE

"And be thankful." Colossians 3:15b

MATERIALS:
Solid, round 1" thick Styrofoam™ base
Tan felt
Scissors
Natural materials (small pinecones, nuts in shells, acorns, seedpods, dried weeds, etc.)
Fall-colored artificial silk-like leaves
Two small, wiggle eyes
Brown chenille wire
Craft glue or low-temperature glue gun and glue sticks
Fall-colored ribbon (brown or gold, 1" wide and 20" long)
Craft feathers
Toothpick
Construction paper scraps
Fine-line markers
Transparent tape

INSTRUCTIONS:
1. Gather natural items to make a centerpiece.
2. Glue a circle of tan-colored felt on the top of the Styrofoam™ base. (If using the glue gun, ask an adult for help.)
3. Make a turkey to glue in the center of the base. Use a small pinecone for the turkey's body. Make the turkey's neck and head from a chenille wire. Glue on wiggle eyes and a beak cut from paper. Make the tail from craft feathers and a large artificial maple leaf.
4. Glue the natural items and leaves on the Styrofoam™ base in an arrangement.
5. Make a little sign from construction paper that says "Be thankful!" Tape a toothpick to the back of the sign and stick it into the Styrofoam™.
6. Place the centerpiece on the Thanksgiving dinner table.

OTHER IDEAS:
- Make a bigger centerpiece, using a larger Styrofoam™ base.
- Make several centerpieces, and give them to a nursing home to brighten the residents' tables for their Thanksgiving meal.

THANKSGIVING NAPKIN HOLDERS

"But thanks be to God!" 1 Corinthians 15:57a

MATERIALS:
Empty cardboard paper towel tube
Ruler
Scissors
Fall-colored felt or construction paper scraps (brown, tan, gold, orange, etc.)
Fine-line marker
Decorative trims (narrow ribbon, autumn and Thanksgiving stickers, dried wheat or weeds, tiny nuts, kernels of Indian corn, etc.)
Craft glue
Napkins (plain or with a Thanksgiving design)

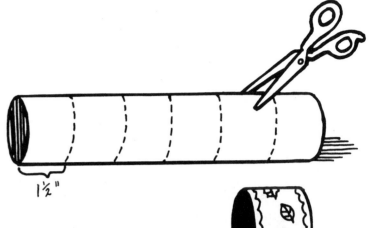

INSTRUCTIONS:
1. Measure and cut 1½" wide rings from a cardboard tube. Cut one for everyone who will attend your family's Thanksgiving dinner.
2. Cover the inside and outside of each ring with construction paper or felt.
3. Write "Give thanks!" on each ring.
4. Decorate the napkin rings with interesting trims so each one looks unique.
5. Roll up paper or cloth napkins and insert one into each napkin holder. Place them on the table where people will eat the Thanksgiving meal.

OTHER IDEA:
- Make extra napkin holders to give to homeless shelters serving hungry people on Thanksgiving. (These people will appreciate knowing that someone cared enough to make napkin holders just for them!)

TURKEY NUT CUPS

"Give thanks in all circumstances." 1 Thessalonians 5:18a

MATERIALS:
Turkey head and neck pattern on this page
Small paper nut cup
Construction paper or colored craft foam
Scissors
Lightweight cardboard
Felt scraps
Two tiny wiggle eyes
Transparent tape
Craft glue or low-temperature glue gun and glue sticks
Fine-line marker
Small treats (chocolate candies, candy corn, nuts, trail mix, raisins, etc.)

INSTRUCTIONS:
1. Make a copy of the turkey head and neck on this page. Cut it out and trace around the pattern on cardboard.
2. Cut out the cardboard, and cover it on both sides with construction paper or felt.
3. Cut a beak from craft foam, paper, or felt. Glue the beak and wiggle eyes to the turkey's head. (If using the glue gun, ask an adult for help.) Tape or glue the neck to the nut cup.
4. Cut five tail feathers in a variety of different colors from craft foam, felt, or paper. If using felt or paper, glue the feathers to cardboard to make them sturdier.
5. Write this sentence with one word on each feather "Thank you, Lord, for everything!"
6. Glue the feathers, overlapping slightly, and spread out to form a fan-shaped tail on the back of the nut cup. (Make sure the words on the feathers are readable and in correct order.)
7. Fill each nut cup with treats, such as nuts or candies.
8. Make enough nut cups to use as party favors. Place one next to the plate of each person who attends your family's Thanksgiving dinner.

OTHER IDEAS:
- You and your family, friends, or classmates can make these nut cups to deliver to shut-in elderly neighbors and other friends on Thanksgiving.
- Make extra nut cups to give to a convalescent home or to the children's ward of a hospital. They can be tray favors for patients on Thanksgiving.

THANKSGIVING PLACE CARDS

"Give thanks to him and praise his name." Psalm 100:4b

MATERIALS:
3" x 5" unlined index cards
Scissors
Fine-line markers
Ink stamp pad (in a fall color such as brown or orange)
Tiny stickers (autumn leaves, Thanksgiving decorations, etc.)

INSTRUCTIONS:
1. Fold 3" x 5" cards in half to make place cards. To make smaller place cards, cut the cards in half and fold.
2. Make a place card for every family member and guest who will attend your family's Thanksgiving dinner.
3. On one side of the place card, write the name of a person who will be at your dinner. You may wish to draw a small picture of that person on the card.
4. Decorate the other side of each card with fall stickers.
5. You may prefer to make a thumbprint by pressing your thumb on an ink stamp pad and then on each card. Let the ink dry; then draw details on the thumbprint to make a tiny turkey.
6. Next to the picture write a phrase, such as "Praise the Lord," to remind everyone why we celebrate Thanksgiving.
7. Find out if the adults who are planning the meal have a specific seating arrangement planned. Put a place card at each person's dinner plate so everyone will know where to sit. The personalized cards will also make each guest feel welcome as you celebrate together.

THANKSGIVING PLACE MATS

Make this project to help your family think about why they should be thankful to God.

MATERIALS:
9" x 12" sheets of construction paper (in fall colors such as orange, tan, yellow, etc.)
Flat aluminum pan or Styrofoam™ meat tray
Poster paint (in fall colors which contrast with construction paper colors)
Crayons and markers
Scissors
Thanksgiving or fall stickers
Clear adhesive plastic

INSTRUCTIONS:
1. Cut 1½" slits to make fringe along the 9" sides of each 9" x 12" sheet of construction paper. These will be the side edges of each place mat.
2. Plan to make one place mat for each family member and guest who will attend your family's Thanksgiving dinner. You may want to use a variety of colors so the place mats will all look different.
3. Pour a small amount of paint into a flat container such as an aluminum pan or Styrofoam™ meat tray.
4. Place the palm of your hand and fingers in the paint. Then press your entire palm and fingers on the paper to make a handprint. While making the print, keep your thumb slightly separate from your fingers. (If you don't have any paint, ask someone to help you use a pen to trace around your hand.)
5. After it dries, decorate the handprint to look like a Thanksgiving turkey with the thumbprint becoming the turkey's head and the fingerprints becoming the turkey's feathers.
6. On the turkey's body write "My many blessings!" On the feathers, write some of the blessings in your life, for example, home, food, family, and friends.
7. Decorate the rest of the place mat with fall stickers and words, such as "Thanks, Lord!"
8. Cover each place mat with clear adhesive plastic so it can be used not only for this Thanksgiving but also for future celebrations.

ADVENT CALENDAR

"For to us a child is born, to us a son is given."   Isaiah 9:6a

MATERIALS:
18" x 36" rectangle of felt (dark or royal blue)
Patterns (pages 82-83)
Pinking shears
Scissors
Crayons, markers, or colored pencils
Lightweight cardboard or old manila folders
Craft glue
Clear adhesive plastic
Fabric scraps (fake fur, burlap, etc.)
Cotton balls
Velcro™ dot fasteners
Heavy yarn or cord
Glitter or glitter pens
1/4" thick wooden dowel (24" long)
Two thumbtacks

INSTRUCTIONS:
1. Copy the patterns on pages 82-83.
2. Color and cut out the figures. Decorate them with glitter and fabric scraps. Glue them on pieces of cardboard or scraps from old manila folders to make the figures sturdier. Trim the edges.
3. Cover the figures with clear adhesive plastic, and trim the edges. Glue cotton on the lambs.
4. Cut felt to suggested size using scissors or pinking shears.
5. Fold up and glue the bottom to make a pocket approximately 6" deep. Glue a vertical divider down the center of the pocket so it won't flop down. Cut and glue letters on the pocket to spell NOEL, a French Christmas greeting.
6. Notch the top edge of the banner as shown. Glue the top edge of the felt over the dowel.
7. Tie yarn or cord to the dowel so you can hang up the calendar. Push thumbtacks into the dowel to keep the yarn or cord in place.
8. Cut a simple stable outline from brown felt. Glue it to the calendar felt.
9. Attach a Velcro™ dot to each of the nativity figures and on the calendar where you plan to place the figures.
10. Hang the calendar on the wall. Place the figures in the pocket. (If the Velcro™ sticks to the felt, line the pocket with paper cut from manila folders.) On each of the twenty-five days of December, including Christmas, pull a figure out and add it to the calendar. You may want to wait until Christmas Day to add the baby Jesus figure.

ADVENT WREATH

Advent is a time of preparation for the celebration of Christ's birth. We celebrate Advent during the four weeks before Christmas. Advent, also, reminds us that Christ will return to earth someday!

MATERIALS:
Advent wreath patterns (page 85)
Three purple taper candles
Pink taper candle
Wide-based, large white candle
Round Styrofoam™ base, 2" thick and 18" wide
Evergreen branches (real or artificial)
Bow
Scissors
Transparent tape
Crayons and fine-line markers
Glitter glue
Clear adhesive plastic
Bible
Matches
Toothpicks

INSTRUCTIONS:
1. Push the large white candle into the center of the Styrofoam™ base.
2. Push the other candles into the Styrofoam™ in a circle around the white candle.
3. Place evergreen branches around the candles covering the Styrofoam™.
4. Place a bow in front of the wreath.
5. Copy the patterns on page 85. Color and cut them out. Decorate the stars in the pictures with glitter glue to make them sparkle.
6. Glue the Scripture verses and explanation copy on the backs of the pictures.
7. Cover each picture with clear adhesive plastic, and trim the edges.
8. Tape a toothpick to the back of each picture.
9. Push each toothpick into the Styrofoam™ so that the picture appears at the base of each candle. The third candles (shepherd's candle) should be the pink "joy" candle, and the center white candle should be labeled with the Christ Child picture. (Make sure the pictures aren't too close to the candle where hot wax might drip down.)
10. On each of the four Sundays before Christmas Day, light another candle and the ones which have already been lit. Light the candles in proper order, and read the Scripture verses. Discuss the meaning of the wreath and each candle. On Christmas Eve and Christmas Day, light all the candles. (If the day you plan to light the final candle is a Sunday, light the fourth candle for the first time with the Christ candle.)
11. This celebration may be done in a classroom, church, or home. You may want to turn off the lights and sing Christmas carols when you light the Christ candle.

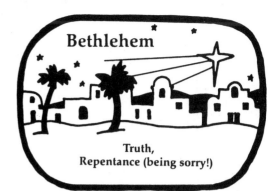

Isaiah 52:7; Isaiah 9:1-7; John 1:5-9

1. The first candle reminds us of the hope of the prophets. They spoke of the coming of the Messiah. Christ's birth made their words come true.

Isaiah 40:1-9; Luke 2:1-7

2. The second candle reminds us of the truth which shines when we are sorry for our sins. It symbolizes the preparations that must be made to receive Christ properly.

Luke 2:8-18

3. The third candle reminds us of the joy of the shepherds. When they heard about Christ's birth, they were filled with joy and worshiped Him. They shared the Good News of His birth with others as we should do.

Luke 2:9-14; John 3:16; 1 John 4:7-10

4. The fourth candle reminds us of the love that the angels proclaimed when Christ was born, and of Christ's return to earth. (Sometimes the fourth candle is named after the wise men who followed the star to find Christ. Draw your own picture and choose appropriate Bible verses about wisdom if you decide to use that symbol instead of the angels and love.)

Luke 2:1-20; 1 John 3:2-3

5. The white candle represents Christ's purity (clean and without sin). This Christ Child candle represents the Savior who brought light to the world and came so that we can live with Him forever.

MANGER SCENE MAILBOX

"I bring you good news of great joy . . . A Savior has been born to you; he is Christ the Lord . . . You will find a baby wrapped in cloths and lying in a manger." Luke 2:10b-12

MATERIALS:
Sturdy, medium-sized cardboard box
Construction paper
Scissors
Glue
Transparent tape
Crayons or markers
Glitter, glitter pens, or metallic star stickers
Fabric scraps
Cotton balls
Yarn
Hole punch
Ribbon or bow

INSTRUCTIONS:
1. Cut a box so that the front and back sides are peaked like a roof, with the back side slightly taller. Cut the sides straight across like the tops of walls as shown.
2. Cover the inside and outside of the box with construction paper. (You may want to cover the outside with light brown to be the stable and the inside to be dark blue or black like the night sky.)
3. Draw a stable and manger scene on the outside front as shown. You may want to use the patterns on pages 82-83.
4. Glue scraps of fabric on the people's clothing. Use yarn for hair and hay. Glue cotton balls on the sheep.
5. Write "Good News!" on the front of the box.
6. Decorate the inside back of the box with glitter or star stickers to look like the night sky. You may want to cut angels out of construction paper to add to the sky.
7. Punch a hole near the top back of the box if you want to hang it up. You may prefer to set it on a table.
8. Attach a bow to the box to decorate it.
9. Use this project as a mailbox to store Christmas cards waiting to be mailed or cards your family receives.

CHRISTMAS GUESTS HAND TOWEL

"Offer hospitality to one another." 1 Peter 4:9a

MATERIALS:
Muslin fabric (approximately 6" x 20")
Scissors
Wax crayons
Iron and ironing board
Newspapers
Rickrack trim
Liquid antifray solution for fabric
Washable glitter paint for fabric
Needle and thread or craft glue

INSTRUCTIONS:
1. Snip the bottom edges of the fabric to make fringe 1/2" long and 1/4" wide.
2. Using crayons, draw a Christmas design such as a manger scene on the fabric.
3. Place the fabric between a folded sheet of newspaper. Set an iron on a low temperature. With an adult's help, iron over the newspaper. You may need to use several sheets of newspaper as the crayon wax design soaks through. When the design shows through slightly on the back side of the fabric, you'll know the crayon design is permanently set.
4. To keep the edges from fraying, use an antifray solution which you can buy at a fabric shop. Spread the solution on the edges. It will harden and dry clear.
5. You may prefer to ask an adult to help you hem the sides and sew rickrack trim along the bottom just above the fringe. If you plan to use the towel only as a decoration and don't plan to wash it, you may glue on the trim.
6. Hang up the towel for guests, or use it as a decorative accessory in a kitchen or bathroom.

PAPER PLATE MOBILE

"My soul glorifies the Lord and my spirit rejoices in God my Savior." Luke 1:46-47

MATERIALS:
Patterns (page 89)
Paper plate
Crayons or markers
Scissors
Stapler and staples
Transparent tape
Yarn or string
Hole punch
Construction paper scraps
Glitter glue
Decorative stickers such as metallic stars
Clear adhesive plastic

INSTRUCTIONS:
1. Copy the Christmas symbols on page 89.
2. Color the symbols and cut them out on the round, heavy outlines.
3. Cover the symbols with clear adhesive plastic.
4. Slit a paper plate from one side to the middle (the radius of the circle).
5. Roll the plate into a cone shape. Overlap the edges, and staple or tape them to make a cone.
6. Cut the tip off the top of the cone. Through the hole, insert a piece of yarn or string long enough to hang below the cone and hold three symbols. Keep some yarn above the top of the cone for a hanger. Tape the yarn in place.
7. Punch holes in the symbols and hang them from the yarn, or tape the symbols to the yarn.
8. Attach other shorter pieces of yarn to the cone, and hang the rest of the symbols. (Place the symbols on all sides of the cone so the mobile stays balanced and doesn't tip to one side.)
9. Cover the backs of the symbols with construction paper if you taped them to the yarn. Make more symbols of your own to add to the mobile.
10. Decorate the cone and symbols with glitter, stickers, and designs cut from scraps of paper. Write on the cone "Celebrate!" and "Happy Birthday, Jesus!"
11. Hang up the mobile as a decoration for the Christmas season or for a holiday party.

NATIVITY SCENE FIGURES

"So they [the shepherds] . . . found Mary and Joseph, and the baby, who was lying in the manger."
                                                                            Luke 2:16

MATERIALS:
Styrofoam™ cups (16 oz. size)
Styrofoam™ balls (3" diameter size)
Craft glue
Fabrics (earth tone colors such as brown and beige)
Scissors
Yarn or twine
12" chenille wires or pipe cleaners (brown, tan, or pink)
Medium-sized wiggle eyes
Construction paper
Felt and yarn scraps
Raffia or bits of dried straw
Cotton balls
Small box

INSTRUCTIONS:
1. Turn Styrofoam™ cups upside down to make figures for a nativity scene.
2. Plan to make Mary, Joseph, and others such as shepherds and wise men.
3. Bend pink or tan chenille wires around the cup bodies to make arms. Twist the ends of the wires to make hands.
4. Drape fabric over the bodies and arms, and glue it on to make clothing.
5. Tie yarn or twine around the figures' waists to make belts.
6. Make staffs for Joseph and the shepherds by breaking off and bending brown chenille wires. Bend hands around to hold the staffs.
7. Glue Styrofoam™ balls on for heads.
8. Make head coverings by gluing on fabric and tying yarn or cord around it.
9. Glue wiggle eyes on the heads. Make other details such as mouths and noses from paper, felt, or yarn scraps.
10. Make a manger from a small box covered with brown paper. Fill it with raffia or straw.
11. Make a little doll from scraps of felt or fabric. Stuff it with a bit of cotton, and glue the edges shut. Place the doll in the manger bed to represent Baby Jesus.
12. Place this display on a table during the Advent season.

STYROFOAM™ CUP NATIVITY ANIMALS

"This will be a sign to you: You will find a baby wrapped in cloths and lying in a manger."

Luke 2:12

MATERIALS:
White Styrofoam™ cups (6.4-oz and 16-oz sizes)
Plain white paper or plastic cups (3-oz bathroom or kitchen dispenser size)
Poster paints (gray, brown, pink, etc.)
Liquid dishwashing detergent
Paintbrushes
Newspapers
Paint smock or large, old shirt
Low-temperature glue gun and glue sticks
Scissors
Craft glue
Wiggle eyes and plastic eyelashes
Yarn or twine
Felt or construction paper scraps
Cotton balls

INSTRUCTIONS:
1. Make animals from Styrofoam™ cups to use with other nativity figures described on page 90.
2. Make animals, such as a donkey, camel, sheep, and goat.
3. Use a low-temperature glue gun to glue together large and small cups. Use large cups for bodies and medium cups for legs, necks, and heads. For smaller animals, such as sheep or goats, use smaller cups. Let the glue dry.
4. Mix a small amount of dishwashing liquid with a larger amount of paint so the paint will stick to the Styrofoam™. Cover your work area with newspapers, and wear a paint smock or old shirt to protect your clothing as you paint the animals.
5. Cover the open ends of the cups by gluing on circles of paper to match the colors of the animals.
6. Make other details by cutting out paper ears, eyelashes, tails, etc., and gluing them on the cups.
7. You may prefer to use wiggle eyes and plastic eyelashes, and yarn for tails, manes, etc.
8. Glue cotton on white cups to make lambs.

CHRISTMAS LAMB CARD

"And there were shepherds living out in the fields nearby, keeping watch over their flocks at night . . . the angel said to them, . . . 'A Savior has been born to you; he is Christ the Lord.'"

Luke 2:8, 10a, 11

MATERIALS:
Lamb pattern (pages 93-94)
Scissors
White heavy paper or lightweight poster board
Cotton balls
Glue or glue stick
Crayons or markers
Two wiggle eyes
Small jingle bell
Glitter
Small pink pom-pom ball
Narrow yarn or ribbon
Hole punch

INSTRUCTIONS:
1. Copy the front and back sides of the lamb pattern on pages 93-94.
2. Have an adult help you cut around the tail and ears. Fold forward on the broken lines. Curl the tail and ears slightly so they stand out from the rest of the body, giving a three-dimensional effect.
3. Glue the pattern pieces to white heavy paper or lightweight poster board, leaving the ears and tail unglued.
4. Cut around the outside edges of the lamb's body.
5. Punch holes, as indicated, along the top of the two body pieces.
6. Place the blank sides of the body pieces together. Lace a piece of yarn or ribbon through the holes, and tie the ends together to make a greeting card.
7. Fold forward on the broken line between the punched holes and press gently on the folded edge to open the card.
8. Inside the card, draw a picture of the shepherds watching their sheep on the first Christmas.
9. Write a greeting inside the card, such as "Have a blessed Christmas!"
10. Color details such as the lamb's face. Add details by gluing cotton on the body, a pink pom-pom on the nose, a bell around the neck, glitter on the bow around the neck, and wiggle eyes.
11. Give this card to a friend, or display it as a stand-up decoration in your home during the Christmas season.

STIFFENED FABRIC ORNAMENTS AND GIFTS

"We saw his star in the east and have come to worship him." Matthew 2:2b

MATERIALS:
Textured burlap or heavy cotton material
Scissors
Liquid fabric stiffener (from fabric or craft shops)
Waxed paper
Decorative trims (ribbon, metallic rickrack, jingle bells, sequins, glitter, etc.)
Craft glue
Hole punch (to make hanging ornaments)
Magnetic tape or small magnets and miniature clothespin (to make a refrigerator magnet)

INSTRUCTIONS:
1. Cut Christmas designs such as stars and bells from fabric.
2. Soak the fabric in liquid stiffener solution.
3. Wring out the excess liquid and place the designs flat on waxed paper. Let the projects dry thoroughly which may take several days.
4. Glue trims on the front of each project to decorate it. Let the glue dry.
5. Punch a hole in the top of each project to make an ornament. Tie ribbon through the hole to hang up the ornament.
6. To make a decorative magnet, glue the project to a small clothespin. Attach magnetic tape or a small magnet to the back of the clothespin. When it dries, give it as a gift to attach memos or a tiny notepad to a metal surface such as a file cabinet or refrigerator.

OTHER IDEAS:
- Rather than using fabric stiffener, glue projects to lightweight cardboard to make them sturdier.
- Trace around Christmas cookie cutters to make simple shapes.

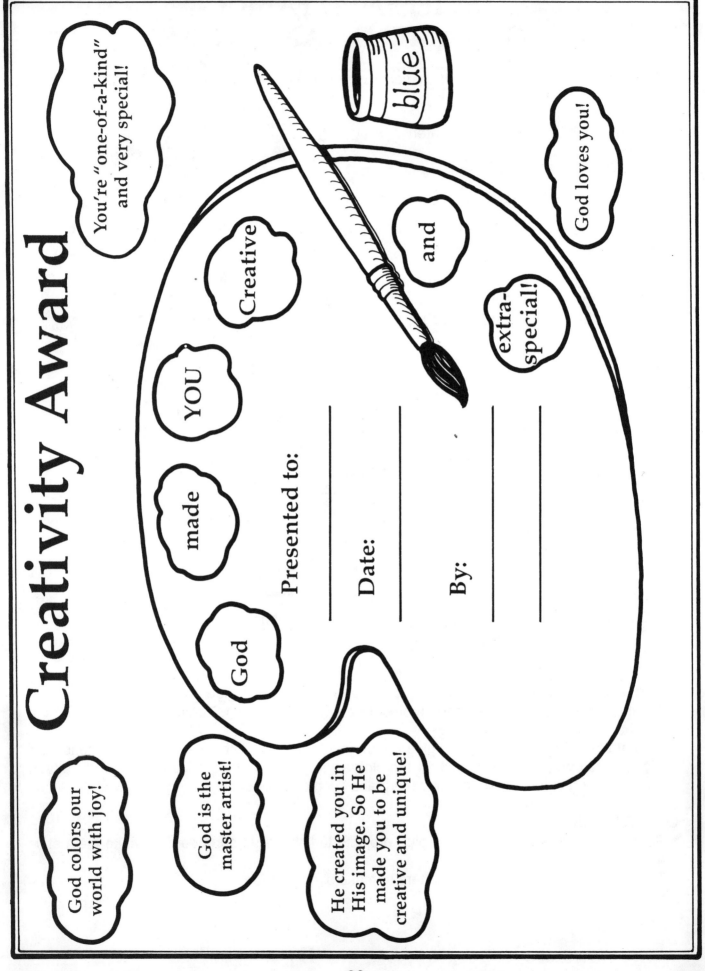